Social and Emotional
Learning in Action

Social and Emotional Learning in Action

Experiential Activities to Positively Impact School Climate

Tara Flippo

ROWMAN & LITTLEFIELD
Lanham • Boulder • New York • London

Published by Rowman & Littlefield
A wholly owned subsidary of The Rowman & Littlefield Publishing Group, Inc.
4501 Forbes Boulevard, Suite 200, Lanham, Maryland 20706
www.rowman.com

Unit A, Whitacre Mews, 26-34 Stannary Street, London SE11 4AB

British Library Cataloguing in Publication Information Available

Library of Congress Cataloging-in-Publication Data

Names: Flippo, Tara, 1972– author.
Title: Social and emotional learning in action : experiential activities to positively
    impact school climate / Tara Flippo.
Description: Lanham : Rowman & Littlefield, [2016] | Includes bibliographical
    references.
Identifiers: LCCN 2015040434 (print) | LCCN 2015051342 (ebook) |
    ISBN 9781475820829 (pbk. : alk. paper) | ISBN 9781475820836 (electronic)
Subjects: LCSH: Experiential learning. | Social learning. | Affective education. |
    Activity programs in education.
Classification: LCC LB1027.23 .F585 2016 (print) | LCC LB1027.23 (ebook) |
    DDC 370.15/34–dc23 LC record available at http://lccn.loc.gov/2015040434

♾™ The paper used in this publication meets the minimum requirements
of American National Standard for Information Sciences—Permanence
of Paper for Printed Library Materials, ANSI/NISO Z39.48-1992.

Printed in the United States of America

Contents

Foreword   xi

Preface   xiii

Acknowledgments   xvii

Introduction   xix

Lesson 1   Community Building: Getting to Know One Another   1
     Program Introduction   1
     Bumpity Bump Bump   1
     Commonalities   2
     Categories   2

Lesson 2   Community Building: Finding Connection and Commonality   4
     Crosstown Connection   4
     What's in a Name?   5
     Have You Ever   5

Lesson 3   Community Building: Full Value and Challenge by Choice   7
     Knee Tag   7
     Comfort Zones   8
     Full Value Concepts   9
     Group Juggle   10

Lesson 4   Community Building and Full Value Contract: Developing Group Norms
     for the Classroom   11
     Full Value Speed Rabbit   11
     The Being   12
     Decision Thumbs   13

Lesson 5   Trust: Trust Sequence I   15
     Look Up, Look Down   15
     Robot   16
     Paired Trust Walk   17

	Sherpa Walk	17
	Debrief: Full Value Contract	18
Lesson 6	Trust: Trust Sequence II	20
	Everybody Up	20
	Trust Leans	21
	Wind in the Willows	21
	Debrief: Pair Share	22
Lesson 7	Trust: Trust Sequence III	24
	Hog Call	24
	Trust Wave	25
	Trust Run	26
	Debrief: Woofs and Wags	26
Lesson 8	Goal Setting: Kaizen: The Art of Continual Improvement	27
	Moonball	27
	On Target	28
	Debrief: Efficiency/Effectiveness Odometer	29
Lesson 9	Communication: Effective Communication Principles	30
	Elevator Air	30
	Communication Breakdown	31
	Debrief: Nuggets	32
Lesson 10	Communication: Expressing Emotions	34
	Creating a Feelings Chart	34
	Emotion Charades	35
	Balloon Trolleys	36
	Debrief: Small Group Questions	37
Lesson 11	Communication: Giving and Receiving Feedback	38
	Caught Ya Peekin'	38
	Lego Statue	39
	Debrief: Plus/Delta	40
Lesson 12	Problem Solving: Individual Contributions to Group Success	41
	Salt and Pepper	41
	Turnstile	42
	1, 2, 3 = 20	42
	Debrief: Pass the Knot	43
Lesson 13	Problem Solving: Introduce ABCDE Model	44
	Silent Lineup	44
	Warp Speed	44
	Star Wars	45
	Debrief: Continuum	46

Lesson 14 Problem Solving: Applying the ABCDE Model 48
RPS World Campionship 48
Group Blackjack 48
Change Up 49
Debrief: Deck of Cards 50

Lesson 15 Reflection: Review Semester and Celebrate Highlights 51
Who Am I? 51
Virtual Slide Show 52
Debrief: Did Ya? 52

Lesson 16 Regroup: Full Value Contract: Semester Review 54
Gotcha FVC Review 54
Stargate 55
Debrief: The Being Revisited 56

Lesson 17 Goal Setting: Setting Behavioral Goals for the Semester 57
How Do You Do? 57
I'm Ok, You're Ok Tag 58
Goal Mapping 59
Debrief: Gallery Walk of Goals 59

Lesson 18 Healthy Relationships: Awareness of Personal Qualities 61
My Qualities 61
Stepping Stone 62
Debrief: Small Group Questions 62

Lesson 19 Healthy Relationships: Consensus 64
Velcro Circle 64
Blind Shape 65
Blind Polygon 65
Debrief: One-Word Whip 66

Lesson 20 Healthy Relationships: Empathy 67
Balloon Frantic 67
Protector 68
Debrief: Pair Share 69

Lesson 21 Healthy Relationships: Trust Sequence IV 70
Everybody's Up 70
Levitation 71
Debrief: Continuum 71

Lesson 22 Healthy Relationships: Negotiation 73
Psychic Handshake 73
Orient the Square 74

	Negotiation Square	74
	Debrief: Human Camera	75
Lesson 23	Goal Setting: Evaluating Goals and Setting Long-Term Goals	77
	Goal Pair Share	77
	Mass Pass	77
	Debrief: Bucket Voting	78
Lesson 24	Leadership: What Is Leadership?	80
	Car and Driver	80
	Don't Break the Ice	81
	Debrief: Leadership Pi Chart	82
Lesson 25	Leadership: Leadership and Followership	83
	Front/Back/Left/Right	83
	Instigator	83
	Pitfall	84
	Debrief: Pitfall Object	85
Lesson 26	Problem Solving: Review ABCDE Model	86
	Your Add	86
	Keypunch	87
	Debrief: Plus/Delta	88
Lesson 27	Problem Solving: Defining Teamwork	89
	Circle the Circle	89
	Portable Porthole	90
	Debrief: Passenger, Crew, Captain	90
Lesson 28	Problem Solving: How I (and Others) Contribute to Our Team	91
	Triangle Tag	91
	Alphabet Soup—Fastback	92
	Debrief: Tic-Tac-Toe	93
Lesson 29	Communication: Effective Communication	95
	Back-to-Back Draw	95
	Bridge It	96
	Debrief: Headliners	97
Lesson 30	Problem Solving: Performing as a Team	98
	Tarp Toss	98
	Turn Over a New Leaf	99
	Debrief: Concentric Circles	99
Lesson 31	Problem Solving: Decision Making	101
	Team Tag	101
	Knot My Problem	102
	Debrief: Pass the Knot	102

Lesson 32	Problem Solving: Competition vs. Cooperation	104
	Thumb Wrestling	104
	Rob the Nest/Share the Wealth	105
	Debrief: Hoop Scoot	106
Lesson 33	Problem Solving: Efficiency and Effectiveness	107
	Evolution	107
	Toxic Waste	108
	Debrief: Pipe Cleaners	109
Lesson 34	Goal Setting: Long-Term Goals	110
	Transformer Tag	110
	Pathways	111
	Debrief: Small Group Questions	112
Lesson 35	Problem Solving: Final Group Challenge	113
	Great Egg Drop	113
	Debrief: Full Value Contract	114
Lesson 36	Closure: Review Semester and Celebrate Highlights	115
	Tool Kit	115
	Warm Fuzzies	116
	Letter to Self	116
Appendix A	Have Your Ever? Cards	119
Appendix B	Efficiency and Effectiveness Odometers	125
Appendix C	On Target Rules	129
Appendix D	Feelings Chart	131
Appendix E	Warp Speed Rules	133
Appendix F	ABCDE Problem Solving	135
Appendix G	SELA Skill Cards	137
Appendix H	Goal Mapping Worksheet	139
Appendix I	My Qualities Cards	141
Appendix J	Keypunch Rules	145
Appendix K	Plus/Delta Worksheet	147
Appendix L	Back-to-Back Draw	149
Appendix M	Original Source for Previously Published Activities	153
Appendix N	SELA Equipment Purchase Lists	161

Appendix O   SELA Logic Model   165

References   167

About the Author   169

Foreword

I first met Tara in the mid-1990s on board a 30-foot sailing vessel in the Boston Harbor. We were leading wilderness trips for adolescent girls with Outward Bound. We had lots in common: each of us was passionate about bringing youth outdoors to empower them through new skill development and experience. It was an exciting time. Daniel Goleman had just published his groundbreaking *Emotional Intelligence*, and the Collaborative for Academic, Social and Emotional Learning (then called Collaborative for Advancement of SEL) had been founded. After those exhilarating Outward Bound days, our paths diverged, yet Tara and I continued on parallel journeys, working with youth and contributing to the new field of SEL.

In my roles as classroom teacher, wilderness instructor, graduate student, SEL trainer/consultant, school counselor, and parent, I heard firsthand the hopes, needs, and worries kids carry with them. While some of these concerns have stayed the same over time, some have morphed as the world has sped up and become hyperconnected. Now, peer interactions can happen 24/7 on social media, adding a whole new dimension to communication. Simultaneously, there are reports of unprecedented levels of isolation, anxiety, depression, and stress in the lives of young people.

Adolescents spend almost half their waking hours in school, and I believe therein lies great potential to counteract isolation, disconnect, and stress. School can offer kids opportunities to connect face-to-face and learn about how their individual talents, needs, and experiences make them unique. Learning about each other and building empathy can be effective antidotes to hostility and stereotyping. For most teachers and principals, creating a positive school climate is a priority in that it ensures the optimal conditions for learning, growth, and transformation. Research confirms the commonsense fact that people learn best when they feel *safe* and *connected*. But how can we ensure that they do?

In my current work as an educational consultant with the Institute for SEL (IFSEL), I interact with educators and administrators from diverse schools around the country. Together we work to strengthen and redesign school-wide systems that support students, faculty, and parents. Through SEL classes and lessons, students learn about themselves and each other, and the direct result is more caring and inclusive communities. In IFSEL's work with schools, we see the diverse ways that SEL lives and breathes, embedded in the structures, norms, and practices of institutions. Many schools have character education programs or life skills classes that teach concepts and ideas valued in their communities, but we hear from teachers over and over: "How do we go beyond talking about ideas and concepts and instead encourage them to *embody* important values such as peace, justice, and cooperation?" SEL and experiential learning offer answers and guidelines, all based on research and practice, and *Social and Emotional Learning in Action* synthesizes that wisdom and makes it accessible to educators.

For the last 30 years, the Browne Center at the University of New Hampshire has worked with thousands of schools, bringing tried-and-true practices from the world of outdoor education and experiential education into the classroom, transforming school culture and motivating students to learn about themselves, build community, and become positive change agents. Under Tara's direction, their work with schools has helped establish emotionally safe, respectful, and inclusive cultures where students can reach their full potential. *Social and Emotional Learning in Action* is a manifestation of short- and long-term youth development/school climate projects that have been implemented for years. Through this exciting new text, *Social and Emotional Learning in Action*, a wider audience of educators and students will benefit from this sound educational approach.

I welcome this book as a practical and timely resource. Schools need the wisdom it contains, and teachers will find it an easy-to-follow guide with tools to empower them to be mentors, guides, and facilitators. The carefully sequenced lessons create safety and trust and pave the way to introduce healthy risk taking, a main developmental task of adolescence. The lessons and activities provide a road map for the journey, with opportunities for reflection, collaboration, and growth. And, most importantly, the activities proactively teach students how to work together and appreciate the value of diversity.

I encourage you to use this book. Try the activities with students. Join the community of educators who are transforming the way people work and communicate by embodying the values of peace, teamwork, integrity, respect, inclusion, and compassion. My hope is that we can each do our part—one classroom, one school at a time—to create a more peaceful and just world.

Elizabeth McLeod, M.Ed.
Educational Consultant and Cofounder
The Institute for Social and Emotional Learning
Montara, California

Preface

DESCRIPTION OF THE BOOK

Social and Emotional Learning in Action (SELA) is an easy-to-use sourcebook facilitated by teaching and/or counseling practitioners primarily in school settings. The pedagogical basis for these lessons is shaped around the research findings of the Collaborative for Academic, Social, and Emotional Learning (CASEL, www.casel.org), which indicates that the inclusion of social and emotional development programs positively affects academic achievement. CASEL has identified five interrelated cognitive, affective, and behavioral competencies: self-awareness, self-management, social awareness, relationship skills, and responsible decision making. SELA lessons address all five competencies. SELA is developmentally sequenced as a yearlong or modular flow—ideal for a class, counseling, or advisory program with a mandate to address these topics. Conversely, an educator could use these as stand-alone lessons to integrate the benefits of experiential and social/emotional learning into the classroom.

SKILL DEVELOPMENT

Through participation in sequenced SELA activities, students will develop and refine their SEL skills and competencies, progressing each month toward different goals and objectives and building upon the previous lesson. These skills and competencies include:

- awareness of personal assets and strengths and how they contribute to group success;
- appropriate expression of feelings, reactions, and ideas;
- awareness of how their actions affect others;
- positive attitudes toward themselves and others;
- mastery of a structured model for decision making and problem solving; and
- understanding of healthy ways of dealing with conflict and stress.

WHO IS THIS BOOK INTENDED FOR?

Educators, middle school and high school teachers, school administrators, school counselors, and youth workers will find this an accessible resource for addressing SEL content with a hands-on approach. The activities in the lessons can positively impact school climate and developmental skills for the 21st century. Additionally it can be a useful resource for meeting school standards relating to social and emotional learning.

ORGANIZATION OF LESSONS

Each of the 36 lessons starts with the intended theme, focus, and activities, including their anticipated time frames and required materials.

Theme: easy-to-search themes. If a teacher wants to use this book out of sequence or in specific sections, the theme will direct the reader to the appropriate lessons. For example, if a lesson on trust fits within that week's larger curricular goals, it would be easy to find the appropriate lessons associated with "trust." A theme may span several lessons.

Focus: keys educators into the focus on that particular lesson. There is a unique focus for each lesson.

Activities: intentionally sequenced within each lesson, as well as in the context of the 36 lessons. Activities are further broken down into objective, setup, framing, procedure, reflection questions, and facilitation tips.

Materials: inventory of materials required for each lesson. In Appendix N is a list of easy-to-source materials from office supplies, sporting goods, or crafts stores. An additional list of specialty materials is included in this appendix, which could be ordered from an experiential training company. The specialty items will be the most expensive aspect of the SELA lessons. However, this is a onetime cost. If your school has a history of using experiential activities, check with the physical education or counseling staff to see if these specialty items are already in the building and could be borrowed.

Most lessons include some form of a warm-up (to get your students focused and "present"), one or more activities (the "meat" of the lesson), and a reflection activity. It is this reflection (or "debrief") that is the heart of a student's skill development. In an ongoing reflective practice, students step back and examine their group and individual process after each activity, identifying behaviors contributing to their success or hindering their performance.

Please note, some activities require prior preparation (e.g., photocopying handouts, cutting out cue cards provided in this guide, etc.).

Equipment must also be gathered and purchased for several of the activities. See the supply list in Appendix N prior to starting to implement these lessons.

WHY EXPERIENTIAL ACTIVITIES?

Experiential activities stimulate insights for your students about behaviors needed to achieve goals. These activities and challenges have been sequenced as progressive lessons for this book. Many of the activities are framed as metaphors for real issues facing students. With years of experience and sound educational pedagogy undergirding them, these dynamic lessons draw on participants' social, cognitive, emotional, and physical abilities. The sequencing of activities is intended to be developmental; that is to say, students will learn about each other and build a sense of community prior to being challenged in problem-solving or trust-building activities.

The SELA activities are drawn from the field of adventure and experiential education and have been adapted from a variety of sources (see Appendix M). In particular, this book has benefited from the extensive curricula and activities of Project Adventure Inc. (www.pa.org).

Acknowledgments

This book is the manifestation of years of hard work by staff of the Browne Center for Innovative Learning (www.brownecenter.com) at the University of New Hampshire. When I arrived as youth and student programs director in 2008, the Browne Center staff had just concluded several years working with multiple middle schools on a year-round program called Edventure. Despite the Edventure curriculum being well received and engaging, I saw a need for revisions which ultimately changed the focus and language, added new activities, and revamped outcomes. The end result was a doubling of the Edventure lessons and changing the entire program schedule and class length. The question now became how to get our lessons—which we knew were vital—into the hands of educators. By 2014, the answer had become clear: move the lessons into a book format.

The book you are now holding represents a manuscript years in the making, a piloted series of lessons, expanded, reworked, and edited for this format. Responses to the lessons from teachers have been overwhelmingly positive, with improved student behavior, a shared common language to reinforce positive behavior, growth in students' skills, transference of these competencies into other classes, and young people assuming new leadership roles.

As I put this book together, I was constantly reminded that I build from a strong foundation. Work from both former and current colleagues allows me an extensive knowledge base of best practices and enables me to tell what works and what doesn't. I have many people to acknowledge. In particular, I want to thank Anthony Berkers, Jo Weston, Sharon England, Melanie Nichols, and Logan Westmoreland on the earlier versions that inspired this current resource book. I also want to thank my supervisor Mark Stailey for his professional coaching. Mark convinced me that a book project was within my reach. He made sure that I prioritized writing over a six-month period.

I also want to thank my mother, Rona Flippo, a seasoned author, whose deep knowledge of publishers and the book manuscript process has been invaluable to me, a first-time author. I could not have accomplished this without the love and support of my parents, Rona and Tyler. And lastly, thanks go to my nieces, nephews, and godson for the inspiration to create important social and emotional learning lessons. Elena, Zoe, Sam, Katelyn, Robert, and Alex: you are all wonderful people.

Introduction

CASE FOR SEL

The Collaborative for Academic Social Emotional Learning (CASEL), founded in 1994, is center stage in its charge for inclusion of SEL in schools. CASEL (2015) describes SEL as

> the process through which children and adults acquire and effectively apply the knowledge, attitudes, and skills necessary to understand and manage emotions, set and achieve positive goals, feel and show empathy for others, establish and maintain positive relationships, and make responsible decisions. (CASEL website)

Since its inception, CASEL's scope and influence has expanded beyond advocacy for inclusion of SEL in schools. These efforts include promotion of teacher grants, legislation, research and its distribution, and influencing school standards.

It is well known that pressures have increased on schools to develop 21st-century skills in their student bodies without sacrificing time for high-stakes exam preparation. However, research shows that Social and Emotional Learning in Action (SELA) students are more likely to attend school and build meaningful connections with peers and staff if engaged in their own learning.

> When educators foster a caring school environment and teach core social skills, a virtuous cycle develops in which positive interactions beget more positive interactions. All of this creates a culture in which students and teachers respect one another and enjoy being together, further strengthening relationships and motivating both students and teachers to do their best. (Edutopia website, 2015)

A 2011 meta-analysis covering over 200 programs and three decades of research provides a compelling case for CASEL's efforts.

> Researchers have found that SEL improves students' attitudes towards themselves and others. Students' participation in classroom-based programs that focused on SEL saw drastic academic gains, with as much as an 11-percentile-point improvement on standardized test scores.
>
> Studies have also shown that improvements in students' SEL skills are also linked to greater self-confidence, mental health, communication skills, and relationships with peers and adults; as well as decreased participation in risky and antisocial behaviors such as drug use, alcohol consumption, and violent acts. (CASEL website)

In addition to stronger peer-to-peer and student-to-school staff relationships, Edutopia (2015) cites several studies showing significant growth of the individual student.

> Self-regulation, the ability to control and manage thoughts, feelings, and behaviors, has been linked to academic achievement in numerous studies. Students who are more self-aware and confident about their learning capacities try harder and persist in the face of challenges. Students who set high academic goals, have self-discipline, motivate themselves, manage stress, and organize their approach to work learn more and get better grades. Finally, students who use problem-solving skills to overcome obstacles and make responsible decisions about studying and completing homework do better academically. (Edutopia website)

SELA, delivered through an experiential approach, only increases its potency. Experiential education has long been known to develop critical thinking, reflection, and lifelong learning skills.

HOW DOES EXPERIENTIAL LEARNING WORK?

When students are given opportunities to learn in authentic situations in school or in the field, like those provided in internships/co-ops and service-learning projects, the learning becomes significantly more powerful. By engaging in formal, guided, authentic experiences, individuals connect their learning to actual experiences, have opportunities for reflection, draw meanings from their reflections, create new learning, and *transfer* their learning into the next experience. Additional benefits include increased motivation for learning and development of *real-world* problem-solving skills which help to create self-directed learners. The acknowledgment of increased engagement, understanding, and enjoyment in learning has led to the development of experiential curriculum, multiple national/international associations and conferences, and countless research articles. It is not necessary to leave the classroom or building to facilitate *authentic* experiential learning.

A list of principles of experiential learning adapted from the leading association on experiential education (www.aee.org) are as follows:

- Learning occurs when carefully chosen activities are supported by reflection, critical analysis, and synthesis.
- Throughout the process, the learner is actively engaged in posing questions, experimenting, solving problems, assuming responsibility, being creative, and constructing meaning.
- Learners are engaged on many levels: intellectually, emotionally, socially, and physically.
- Relationships are both developed and nurtured: learner to self, learner to others, and learner to the world at large.
- Opportunities are nurtured for learners to explore and examine their own values.
- The educators' primary roles include structuring an intentionally sequenced flow of activities, setting boundaries, supporting learners, ensuring physical and emotional safety, and facilitating the reflection process.
- The educator also recognizes and encourages spontaneous opportunities for learning.

The Kolb Cycle of Experiential Learning shows these stages.

Kolb's Cycle of Experiential Learning

CONCRETE EXPERIENCE

Direct participation

ACTIVE EXPERIMENTATION

Testing new ideas/skills

REFLECTIVE OBSERVATION

What happened?

ABSTRACT CONCEPTUALIZATION

Creating meaning from observations

Lesson 1

Community Building

Getting to Know One Another

ACTIVITIES ⚽

1. Program Introduction (5 minutes)
2. Bumpity Bump Bump (10 minutes)
3. Commonalities (15 minutes)
4. Categories (15 minutes)

MATERIALS ✍

• None

---

1. PROGRAM INTRODUCTION (5 MINUTES)

Introduce yourself and tell your students what you expect from their participation in SELA lessons.

2. BUMPITY BUMP BUMP (10 MINUTES)

Objective: A fun game to help students learn one another's names.
Setup: Have your group stand in a circle, placing yourself as the leader in the middle of the circle.
Framing: Say to students: "This game should help us to learn each other's names in a fun, fast-paced game."

1. Explain that the person standing in the middle of the circle can point to anyone in the circle, look them straight in the eye and declare the words "left," "right," "you," or "me."
2. The person pointed at must then call out the name of the person to their left or right, their own name, or the name of the person doing the pointing.
3. Do a few rounds of simple naming without time constraints.
4. Ask students to repeat after you the words "bumpity bump bump."
5. Repeat step 2, but this time add the words "bumpity bump bump" immediately after the left-right-you-me command.
6. The pointee must call out the left-right-you-me name before the pointer finishes saying the last "bump." If they do not, the pointee and the pointer swap positions.

Facilitation Tips
Start your own "bumps" at a slow pace as students will quickly speed the game up.

3. COMMONALITIES (15 MINUTES)

Objective: To discover commonalities with other students.
Setup: Ask the students to arrange themselves in pairs, preferably with someone they don't know well.
Framing: Say to students: "In this activity you will find some commonalities with other people that you didn't already know. As we get to know each other better, we are more likely to work together cooperatively."

1. In pairs, students try to generate a list of things that are common to both of them but which you could not identify by looking at them.
2. Give students a few minutes and then ask the groups to report back a few of the most curious or interesting commonalities they discovered.
3. Variation: Have students swap partners and/or form groups of four.

Facilitation Tips
Commonalities may include speaking the same foreign language, having the same number of siblings, have the same letter starting their last name, etc. This does *not* include things you can see such as wearing glasses, having brown hair, etc.

4. CATEGORIES (15 MINUTES)

Objective: To find more in common with our peers.
Setup: Clear a space in the room so students can walk around freely.
Framing: Say to students: "Here's another activity that will help us learn about one another and build our community."

1. Ask everyone to stand up and then to walk around; explain that you will announce a category (see list or use your own) and that participants should then quickly organize themselves into smaller groups based on the category to which they belong. For example, if you say "favorite ice cream flavor," all chocolate lovers get together, all strawberry, etc.
2. Once everyone is organized into their groups, ask each group to identify itself.
3. Variation: Ask the students to generate categories in which they would like to group together.

Facilitation Tips
Suggested Categories:

- What is your favorite season?
- How many siblings do you have?

- What is your favorite soft drink?
- What color are your eyes?
- What is your favorite sport?
- What's your shoe size?
- What is your favorite music group?
- What's your favorite color?
- If you could own any car, what would it be?
- If you had a superpower, what would it be?

Lesson 2

Community Building
Finding Connection and Commonality

ACTIVITIES ⚽	MATERIALS ✏️
1. Crosstown Connection (10 minutes) 2. What's in a Name? (10 minutes) 3. Have You Ever? (25 minutes)	• Spot markers (one per student) • Have You Ever? statement cards (copy from Appendix A)

1. CROSSTOWN CONNECTION (10 MINUTES)

Objective: A quick, fun warm-up game that allows students to mingle with each other.

Setup: Have your group stand in a circle.

Framing: Say to students: "Greetings are an important way of knowing you are part of a community. We are going to introduce ourselves quickly using a variety of unique handshakes."

1. Have students pair up and greet their partner using a unique handshake (see Facilitation Tips).
2. Have students change to a new partner and get them to introduce each other using a different handshake unique to this new partnership.
3. Remind students that they should remember which handshake is associated with which partner as they will need to find them again.
4. Once students have done three to five handshakes (all with different people), call out a handshake style and have students quickly find their partner and perform that specific handshake.
5. Call out a few of the handshakes in a series so students rush from one partner to another.
6. Variation: Generate your own unique handshakes to share or have the students share their favorite or culturally unique handshake.

Safety Check
Students should be mindful not to run into each other as they race to find their partner.

Facilitation Tips
One point of confusion is having students use the same handshake with multiple peers. Each handshake should only be associated with one other student.

Handshake Examples:

- High Five
- Low Five
- Fist Pump
- Lumberjack: start with a closed fist "thumbs up." Partner grabs thumb and sticks up their own. Stack hands in a similar fashion until all four hands create a "saw." With a good stance, mime a back-and-forth sawing motion.
- Fishtail: Each partner extends one arm in a handshake position. Instead of clasping hands, hands are placed near their partner's elbow and gently slapped in the motion of a fish's tail.
- Dairy Farmer: One partner interlocks their fingers while keeping their thumbs up. Thumbs are rotated down creating the "udders." The other student "milks the udders."
- Businessperson: Both students mime talking on cell phones (pinky and thumb extended) and great each other with a furtive head nod and fist bump.

2. WHAT'S IN A NAME? (10 MINUTES)

Objective: A partnered activity where students discuss their personal background by describing the story and/or origins of their name.

Setup: Have students pair up with a peer they don't know well.

Framing: Say to students: "We all have unique backgrounds and family heritage. This activity is sharing a little about your family by telling the story behind your first and last names. If you have a middle name, that one too."

1. In pairs, ask students to talk about the origins/history of each of their names, how they got them, and where they're from. Tell them that they will introduce their partner and one interesting fact about their name.
2. Give students at least three to four minutes to discuss and then ask the pairs to introduce each other to the group.

3. HAVE YOU EVER? (25 MINUTES)

Objective: To explore common experiences with other student groups.

Setup: Have your group stand in a circle. Put a spot marker at the foot of each person (not including yourself). Add a final spot for yourself (which can be of different color or size) and designate that as the "card-reading spot."

Framing: Ask the class: "Have you ever wondered who in this class has traveled to a foreign country, or who speaks another language, or who has more than four siblings? Now is our chance to learn more about one another."

1. Ask the first Have You Ever? question (Appendix A). Explain to students: "If your answer to the question is yes, then you are to move from your spot to a new spot, but not the spot next

door. If your answer is no, then you are to remain on your spot. One student will end up on the card-reading spot. Once everyone is settled, that person will draw a new card and read the next question."

2. The person in the card-reading spot must move to a new spot regardless of whether he or she did or did not answer "yes" to the question. This assures a new person in the card-reading spot each time.

3. During the activity, you may ask some related follow-up questions to the students who have moved, such as, "What other language do you speak?" or "How many siblings do you have?" If appropriate, you can also have students ask questions of each other: "I'm curious about that."

4. Variation: In addition to using the Have You Ever? cards, students can also choose to create a Have You Ever? statement. The statement must be true about the person making the statement. Emphasize that statements should be appropriate for the group.

Safety Check
Remind students to be mindful of not bumping into one another as they walk to a new spot.

Facilitation Tips
Have You Ever? statement cards (Appendix A): This is a set of starter questions. There are also blank cards that you can fill out prior to the activity. Copy and cut these out. In addition, you may ask students to generate statements during the game.

Follow-Up Questions:

- Were you surprised to see other people move when you did?
- Did you know you had so many things in common with each other? Did you also know there were so many differences?
- What else did you learn doing this activity? What might this mean for our time together?

Lesson 3

Community Building
Full Value and Challenge by Choice

ACTIVITIES ☻	MATERIALS ✎
1. Knee Tag (10 minutes) 2. Comfort Zones (10 minutes) 3. Full Value Concepts (10 minutes) 4. Group Juggle (15 minutes)	• Two ropes • Masking tape and pens (or permanent markers) • Fleece balls (one per student) • Whiteboard or poster board and associated markers

1. KNEE TAG (10 MINUTES)

Objective: To tag other students while trying to not be tagged by others.

Setup: Clear an open space in the class and have students circle up.

Framing: Say to students: "Here's a fun version of tag to warm us up. In Knee Tag, you get to decide when you are playing it safe and when you want to risk moving or tagging another player."

1. Explain that this is a version of "Everybody's It" tag, where everyone is "It" while simultaneously trying to avoid being tagged by anyone else.
2. Demonstrate the two positions in the game:
   • Knees slightly bent and both hands covering knees. In this position, students cannot move or tag anyone, but they are safe from being tagged.
   • Stand with both hands raised (like in a holdup). In this position, students can move and they can tag other students, but they can also be tagged.
3. A score is made when one student tags the undefended kneecap of another student while they were moving or tagging. Naturally, in order to make a tag, a person's hand must leave their knee, so they are vulnerable to attack as well.
4. Variation: Introduce the "hands up" rule. When your group hears you shout, "Hands up," everyone must hold their hands up high and above their head and not defend their knees. They may, of course, choose to lower a hand to make a committed tag of any exposed knees, but

that's it! Shortly after, your call of "hands down" returns people to the status quo, until the next "hands up" and so on.

Safety Check
Watch your head! The focus is all on the knees and hands, thus there may be a tendency to forget about the possibility of bumping heads as people dart about to prevent being tagged.

Facilitation Tips
Later, when talking about Comfort Zones, you can refer to how students chose to make themselves vulnerable (or not) in knee tag as an example of Challenge by Choice.

2. COMFORT ZONES (10 MINUTES)

Objective: To understand the importance of respecting and supporting their own and other students' decisions regarding personal level of challenge.

Setup: Use masking tape or two ropes to create three distinct zones as shown below.

Comfort Zone	Stretch Zone	Panic Zone

Framing: Explain to students the meaning of the different zones of the circles in front of them (see Facilitation Tips).

1. Students will have to move to the "zone" that most appropriately fits with each new question. How do you feel about:
   - spiders?
   - speaking in front of a large group?
   - singing solo in front of a large group?
   - singing in a choir?
   - bungee jumping?
   - heights?
   - confronting a friend about something they did or said?
   - snakes?
   - taking a math test?
   - introducing yourself to someone new?
   - taking a driver's test?
   - coming to class?
2. After each round, have students look around and notice the diversity of responses.
3. You (or the students) may add your own questions.

Facilitation Tips

"When considering the idea of Challenge by Choice, it is helpful to talk about the idea of challenge as well as choice. When we are in our comfort zones, each of us is in a place that is safe and secure. By choosing to step out of our comfort zone to the stretch zone, we are open to new ideas and experiences. We are, in essence, breaking new ground. Although not always easy, this is a place for optimum learning. What we try to avoid is going beyond the stretch zone into the panic zone. The panic zone is a place where learning cannot take place because the threat is too big."

Questions to Explore with Your Students:

- Did everyone usually end up in different places? What does that mean about this class?
- What does it mean when someone chooses to participate in a way that is different from others?
- How can we support the choices that each one of us makes?
- How can we encourage you to step into your stretch zone without putting too much pressure on you?
- What can we do to help you when you are in your panic zone?

3. FULL VALUE CONCEPTS (10 MINUTES)

Objective: To provide students with a "group norms" framework called Full Value Concepts. Our Full Value Concepts will become the behavioral contract that informs our group work and individual commitments around behavior toward the group.

Setup: Have students sit comfortably in a circle.

Framing: Say to students: "Part of the SELA program is 'Full Value.' Full Value Concepts are group commitments to behaviors that are part of a healthy learning community. For each of us, knowing what is expected from each other around acceptable behavior is easier when we have common definitions. What I may mean by showing respect and what you may mean could look very different unless we talk about it."

1. Write the Full Value Concepts on a whiteboard or poster board:
   - Be Here
   - Be Safe
   - Be Honest
   - Set Goals
   - Care for Self and Others
   - Let Go and Move On
2. Give a brief description of what each concept means:
   - Be Here, being fully present
   - Be Safe, physically and emotionally
   - Be Honest, giving and receiving feedback, speaking your own truth
   - Set Goals, attainable and positive

- Care for Self and Others, being a responsible member of the community
- Let Go and Move On, using feedback for growth

3. Next ask your students to generate specific examples of *What does _____ look like?* or *What does _____ sound like?* It may be helpful to keep a running list on the whiteboard. If students give generic answers like "support" or "teamwork," ask them to go further and get very specific (e.g., "What would you be hearing if the group was being supportive?").

4. GROUP JUGGLE (15 MINUTES)

Objective: To review the Full Value Concepts while playing a fun game.

Setup: Arrange participants in a circle, not too close or too far from one another.

Framing: Say to students: "We are going to do an activity that will bring to life our Full Value Concepts. To start, each of you should write, on a piece of masking tape, one Full Value Concept that you feel is very important, or one that you feel may be difficult to follow. I am going to give each one of you a ball to tape your norm onto. The activity will require us to effectively juggle these concepts!"

1. Starting with one ball, develop a throwing pattern following these guidelines:
   - You cannot throw to someone on your immediate right or left.
   - You can only throw and catch once each while developing your pattern.
   - Once everyone has thrown once and caught the ball once, make sure the pattern can be recreated.
   - Practice the pattern more than once.
2. Ask the group to set a goal regarding how many balls they think they can juggle at once (no more than the number of students in the group).
3. Students will now attempt to juggle as many balls as possible without dropping any. Start each group with just few balls and gradually add more.
4. Discussion questions:
   - What happened when a ball was dropped?
   - Is this similar to what we may do when we "drop" a Full Value Concept?
   - Was it difficult to juggle multiple norms?
   - Do we feel confident we can manage our Full Value Concept?

Safety Check
Make sure that rambunctious throws are discouraged.

Facilitation Tips
Some students may have difficulty throwing and catching balls. Be sure to set a positive tone and begin the tossing pattern slowly. Beanie babies or other small plush toys can also be used to make catching easier.

Lesson 4

Community Building and Full Value Contract
Developing Group Norms for the Classroom

ACTIVITIES ⚽	MATERIALS ✏
1. Full Value Speed Rabbit (15 minutes)	• Flip chart paper
2. The Being (30 minutes)	• Masking tape
3. Decision Thumbs (included in The Being)	• Assorted washable markers

1. FULL VALUE SPEED RABBIT (15 MINUTES)

Objective: To review the Full Value Concepts from the last lesson in a fun way.

Setup: Ask the class to stand in a circle, shoulder to shoulder. Have fun with the demonstration of this activity and fully participate with the students to role-model enjoyable, zany behavior. It sets a lighthearted tone and reinforces the message that it is OK to try new things.

Framing: Review the Full Value Concepts shared in the Lesson 3. Say to students: "We will be playing a game using each of the Full Value Concepts":

• Be Here
• Be Safe
• Be Honest
• Set Goals
• Care for Self and Others
• Let Go and Move On

1. Have the class develop a symbol that represents each of the six Full Value Concepts. These "symbols" are composed of three people each (see Facilitation Tips for examples). Have the class practice making the various symbols before the game begins.
2. Choose one person (the leader) to be in the center of the circle. The leader spins around in a circle, then randomly points to someone in the circle and calls out one of the six symbols. The leader then counts to 10.
3. The player who is pointed to becomes the main body of the symbol; the people who are on either side of this player are the two sides. They must try to arrange themselves into the symbol

before the leader finishes counting. If they don't, the part of the symbol that is not in place takes the leader's spot in the middle of the circle. If they are done in time, the leader stays and spins again.

4. Variation: As the group masters the different symbols, add animals and other creative symbols to the game (see Facilitation Tips for examples).

5. Discussion: Have the class split into small groups. Ask each group to discuss one of the Full Value Concepts. Students in each group should answer the question, "How will we know when we are doing our Full Value Concept and when we are not doing it?" Have each group report out to the whole class. As a class, discuss how students will maintain the concepts. Who is responsible for monitoring it?

Facilitation Tips
Symbol Ideas:
Have the class make up their own after you give them a few examples like the following:

- Be Here: Center person stands in a sumo wrestler stance, with hands on hips. Side people each grab one of the wrestler's arms and gently pull, showing that the center person is "here."
- Be Safe: Center person waves a baseball "safe" sign while each of the side people puts a leg in the middle as if sliding into base.
- Let Go and Move On: Center person turns their back while the side people pretend to be letting go of a rope they have been pulling on.
- Elephant: Center person extends left arm down and holds nose with right hand to form a trunk. Side people form ears by facing the center person and making a C shape with their arms.
- Rabbit: Center person uses hands to make rabbit ears on their head. Side people each stand near the center person while making a fast kicking/stepping motion with their legs like a rabbit.

Keep the game fun!
Help each small group get specific about how to behave using their Full Value Concept.

2. THE BEING (30 MINUTES)

Objective: Students will generate specific group behavioral norms and values related to the Full Value Concepts. These are target behaviors for which the group will strive.

Setup: Tape the flip chart pages together to create a canvas big enough to accommodate one group member. Have a student volunteer lie down on the canvas and outline their body.

Framing: Remind students of the Full Value Concepts discussed in the previous activity.

1. On the inside of the outline, students should draw or write behaviors or qualities that exemplify the Full Value Norms and are positive (e.g., friendship, respect, the act of shaking hands).

2. On the outside of the outline, they should draw or write behaviors or qualities that would contravene the Full Value Norms or that damage people's sense of respect and safety (e.g., prejudice, exclusion).

3. Use the Decision Thumbs (see activity 3) to periodically check for consensus on the behaviors and qualities listed in The Being.
4. Once all students are in accord with the behaviors and qualities listed (everybody gives a thumbs-up), have students sign their names inside The Being to show their commitment to the group and the Full Value Concepts.

Facilitation Tips

Encourage people to be creative with their outlines. Dress them up a bit.

Pick one or more of the following questions to deepen the group's reflection about The Being (or come up with your own).

- How might The Being help remind us about making this a safe and respectful classroom?
- When there are issues that occur from the outside of the Being, how can we handle them?
- How can we use the inside attributes while working to diminish the outside attributes?
- Nobody is perfect; having a "goal" provides something for students to strive for. As such, students will not follow the norms at times or will "mess up." Now that our norms have been agreed to, a system of accountability needs to be put in place.

3. DECISION THUMBS

Objective: To practice inclusive and consensual decision making, where all voices are heard and where dissenting opinions are allowed and explored.

1. Review Decision Thumbs options:
   - Thumbs Up—means "I agree with the decision and want to act on it."
   - Thumbs Down—means "I don't agree on the decision and do not want to act on it. I may need more information to go along, or an entirely different solution."
   - Thumb Sideways—means "I don't agree with the decision, but I am OK with acting on it."
2. Ask students to vote on the content of the inside of The Being.
3. If all or most students are Thumbs Up and the remaining students are Thumbs Sideways, the resolution is passed.
4. If even one student votes Thumbs Down, the resolution is not passed. The group needs to hear this (or these) group members, provide more information or clarity on the resolution, or find an entirely different solution.
5. As the group works through people's concerns, a round of Decision Thumbs can be done periodically to check for consensus.

Facilitation Tips

Consensus decision making can be difficult and demands a high level of engagement. When everyone else is voting Thumbs Up, it takes courage to stand with a Thumbs Down. It requires the willingness to be open to other people's ways of seeing the world and a willingness to work toward group success.

If many students either immediately go Thumbs Up and Thumbs Sideways and you think there is a lack of involvement or commitment in the group, open a discussion about this. Reinforce the idea that this is their group and that they are responsible for most of the decisions, success, and failures.

Students can use the Decision Thumbs at any point in SELA lessons when they are trying to make a decision and want to get a quick check on everyone's engagement and concerns.

Lesson 5

Trust

Trust Sequence I

ACTIVITIES ⚽

1. Look Up, Look Down (5 minutes)
2. Robot (10 minutes)
3. Paired Trust Walk (10 minutes)
4. Sherpa Walk (10 minutes)
5. Debrief: Full Value Contract (10 minutes)

MATERIALS ✍

• Blindfolds (one per student)
• The Being Full Value Contract

---

1. LOOK UP, LOOK DOWN (5 MINUTES)

Objective: To form a quick partnership through mutual eye contact.

Setup: Form a circle with students shoulder to shoulder.

Framing: Say to students: "In this game you must commit to look at one person every round. You cannot search around for a new person!"

1. Explain to the group that you are going to be told to either look up or look down. On the command "Look down," everyone is asked to cast their eyes down at the ground, toward their feet. Then, on your command to "Look up," everyone is obliged to lift their gaze to the eye level of other group members. Students must commit to one person only per round.

2. If two people happen to look at each other (i.e., by chance) at the same time, they should exclaim "Aha!"

3. Continue for a few rounds of fun. When you want to split the group into pairings, instruct the students that with the next rounds, in addition to saying "Aha!" the person they "caught" will become their partner for the next activity. As pairing occurs, students break away from their neighbors and depart from the circle.

4. After a pair or more leaves, the next call of "Look down" is issued.

5. Repeat until all students are partnered for the following activity.

Facilitation Tips
If you have an odd number, either join in with the last student or have a group of three.

2. ROBOT (10 MINUTES)

Objective: To direct another group member to move around the room using limited commands.
Setup: Maintain the pairings from the end of the last activity.
Framing: Say to students: "We have on loan today something that is very exciting. We have been asked to test out some very expensive robots! They are the first model of this kind, so they do not have many buttons or controls. We need your help to test them out!"

1. Explain how the robots function by describing the buttons that they come with: Left Turn, Right Turn, Go Forward, Stop, and a two-part Safety Feature!
2. Demonstrate the following with a willing robot volunteer. The Left button is located on the left shoulder of the robot. If this button is pushed, the robot will turn to the left. The Right button is located on the right shoulder.
3. The Go Forward button is located in the middle of the back. Tap this button once and the robot will walk forward.
4. The Stop button is located on the top of the head. Gently tap this once and the robot will stop.
5. The robot has two Safety Features. The first is that it always travels with "bumpers up." Secondly, the robot has an alarm that sounds whenever the robot comes close to an object or another robot.
6. Demonstrate the alarm: "Whoop, whoop, whoop, whoop, whoop."
7. The robots can only travel at walking pace.
8. One student begins as a robot, the other as the operator.
9. Remind students that the robots are very expensive and fragile. So it is very important that they follow all the guidelines. After a few minutes, have the robot and operator switch roles.

Safety Check
Make sure that there is an open space, free of obstacles. In small spaces, you can have the robots only walk heel-to-toe to slow them down.
Make sure that the robots have the Safety function—if they are in danger, they stop moving and exclaim "Whoop whoop whoop!"
Make sure the robots keep their eyes open.

Facilitation Tips
If you have an odd number of students, a group of three can be formed. They can decide if they each want to take turns or if the operator wants to handle two robots at the same time.
If someone does not wish to be touched at all, offer the option of having the operator give verbal directions.

Questions to Ask the Group before Moving on to the Next Activity:

- What was it like to trust someone else to direct you?
- What made it easy for you to follow their directions?
- How did it feel to be responsible for someone else?

3. PAIRED TRUST WALK (10 MINUTES)

Objective: To have students lead each other blindfolded through the classroom, halls, and/or outdoors.

Setup: Maintain the same pairings as in the previous activity or have students choose another partner.

Framing: Say to students: "You've just led your partner using only nonverbal signals. In this activity, you will also be able to use your voice, but your partner will be blindfolded."

1. Show the class different methods for leading someone who cannot see. The person being led can hold hands with the guide, hold the elbow of the guide, or have the guide hold his or her elbow. Or she may not wish to be touched at all but may opt for verbal directions only. The important thing is that each pair discusses how they want to be led.
2. Offer blindfolds for those who want them; if not, students can simply close their eyes.

Safety Check

Blindfolded students should be in the "bumpers up" position (hands out in front with palms facing out). Emphasize that at any time either person in the partnership can stop the activity if he or she feels unsafe.

Facilitation Tips

You can conduct this activity inside the classroom, throughout the school, or outside. A variation is to have students lead their partners to a particular object (tree, chair, painting, etc.) and have them feel it. Later they can try to guess what and where it was.

Sample Questions:

- What did your guide do to gain your trust? Be specific.
- Did you feel your guide took care of your safety? Why or why not?
- Were you more comfortable being led or leading?
- If we did this activity again, what would you do differently to help your partner trust you more?

4. SHERPA WALK (10 MINUTES)

Objective: To have students each lead the entire group on part of a blind group walk.

Setup: Be sure to have a route in mind for the walk. To make it more challenging, you may want a series of twists and turns as well as objects that students will need to step over or under.

Framing: Say to students: "This is another blindfold activity. The entire class will be led on a 'Sherpa Walk.' Who can tell me where the term 'Sherpa' comes from and what they do? During this Sherpa Walk you will have to support each other as you move along. You will be able to have physical contact while you walk, but no talking allowed."

1. Have students get into groups of four to discuss what they will each personally need from the group to make participating in this activity comfortable. Have the groups share what they discussed.
2. Offer blindfolds to students who want them. Encourage others to keep their eyes closed the entire time.
3. Ask the group if they would like to discuss any strategies before proceeding.
4. Ask students to get into a line and put on blindfolds and/or close their eyes.
5. Remind students that there is no talking, but they can be in physical contact with others.
6. When everyone is ready to go, the first student in the line may have their eyes open and/or blindfold off.
7. Show the first student the course you think they should take to match the challenge level desired.
8. Rotate the first student to the back of the line after a couple of minutes to allow for a new leader.

Safety Check
Stop the line and spot students as they move through difficult sections of the walk.
Make sure that you can safely monitor what you are asking students to do; remember, all but one cannot see!

Facilitation Tips
You can ask one or two students to be sighted spotters and observers of the class. These "observers" can provide useful feedback for the group during the debrief.

5. DEBRIEF: FULL VALUE CONTRACT (10 MINUTES)

Objective: To have students reflect on The Being, the Full Value Contract (FVC), and connect it with specific behaviors during the lesson.
Setup: Have students form a circle.
Framing: Say to students: "The Being, our Full Value Contract, isn't just a piece of paper, it's something we can use to help us be a better community and team and to achieve success."

1. Review the FVC with students (Be Here, Be Safe, Be Honest, Set Goals, Care for Self and Others, Let Go and Move On).
2. Ask students to think about which of the concepts the group did best at today and a specific example of when they saw this happening.

3. Ask a few individual students which FVC norm they picked and why.

4. Repeat steps 2 and 3, this time focusing on what the group could most improve on.

Facilitation Tips

Students often need to be coached in giving specific examples. If they are giving a vague example, try asking them, "When did you see that?" or "What specific action made you feel _____?" You do not need to hear from every student on each round.

Lesson 6

Trust
Trust Sequence II

ACTIVITIES ⚽	MATERIALS ✍
1. Everybody Up (10 minutes) 2. Trust Leans (10 minutes) 3. Wind in the Willows (15 minutes) 4. Debrief: Pair Share (10 minutes)	• None

1. EVERYBODY UP (10 MINUTES)

Objective: To stand up back to back from a seated position, working with a partner.

Setup: Ask your students to circle up.

Framing: Say to students: "Last time we explored trust using mostly unsighted activities with guides. Today we are going to try some fun activities where you support one another through holding each other up."

1. Have the group get into pairs.
2. Have each pair stand back to back and link arms. Have them sit on the floor.
3. When they are ready, students can attempt to stand up as a pair.
4. Once they have succeeded, have two pairs join so that the groups are four people, and have them attempt to stand up together.
5. Variation: Pressing backs together without linking arms.

Safety Check

Students with shoulder injuries should be careful when doing the back-to-back version of this activity.

2. TRUST LEANS (10 MINUTES)

Objective: To build trust and have students support each other.

Framing: Say to students: "This is an opportunity to learn and practice correct spotting technique. It is also an opportunity to develop trust between you and your classmates. Think about people in your life whom you support. What is it about that person that allows us to do that? As spotters today, you will each have a chance to be that person who is literally being leaned on for support."

1. Ask participants to find a partner of similar height; same-sex pairs are not essential but often occur.
2. One person is the Faller and one the Catcher. The Catcher stands behind the Faller in the "spotting" position.
3. Faller must adopt the falling posture:
    a. standing upright
    b. feet together
    c. hands across chest, resting on shoulders
    d. keep body stiff (to avoid buckling)
4. Catcher is taught "spotting"
    a. one leg in front of the other
    b. arms extended, with elbows bent and loose
    c. "give" with the weight, taking it mostly through the legs
5. Start with short falls, then slowly add distance in small incremental steps.
6. Establish clear communication calls:
    a. Faller: "I am ready to fall. Are you ready to catch me?"
    b. Catcher: "I am ready to catch you. Fall away."
    c. Faller: "Falling."
    d. Catcher: "OK"
7. If time allows, find a new partner and start the sequence over.

Safety Check

Create a careful, concentrating, respectful tone. Watch out for bravado; focus on trust and care. Reinforce the communication as students sometimes rush through this.

3. WIND IN THE WILLOWS (15 MINUTES)

Objective: To build trust and have group members support each other.

Setup: Ask your students to circle up.

Framing: Say to students: "Because you have done so well in the trust leans, we are ready to go a step further. During this activity you, as the Faller, will need to establish trust between yourself and the rest of the group."

1. With the whole group, one person volunteers to be the "willow" in the middle. The rest of the group stands in "spotter ready" position with one foot forward, hands up. Appropriate stance for the "willow" looks like:
   a. Feet together
   b. Closed eyes (optional)
   c. Arms crossed and hands on shoulders
   d. Body rigid and straight
   e. Establishes contract with group (see below)
   f. "Trust lean" and allows him/herself to be "passed around" the group.

2. The final step before leaning is to create a contract between the "willow" and the group. It can sound like this:
   a. Willow: "I am ready to fall. Are you ready to catch me?"
   b. Group: "We are ready to catch you. Fall away."
   c. Willow: "Falling."
   d. Group: "OK."

Safety Check

Ensure the group is tight, should to shoulder, with arms outstretched. In this position, hands should almost touch the person standing in the middle. This ensures that the initial fall will be very gentle. Gradually the group can ease back to allow a more expansive lean. Distribute large and small people evenly to avoid stress on any one person. Typically, two to three people are hands on at the same time.

Facilitation Tips

The "willow" should allow him/herself to be passed around by the group as long as she/he likes (usually one to two minutes). When he/she has had enough, simply open eyes, stand up, and thank the group.

The quality of the atmosphere and caring will generally determine the proportion of people prepared to volunteer.

4. DEBRIEF: PAIR SHARE (10 MINUTES)

Objective: To have students reflect on the concept of trust and how they experience it in their class and in their lives.

Setup: Have students pair up. Assign pairs randomly (or purposefully) or have students select a partner.

Ask partners to share with each other:

- Do you think we could have done this at the start of our year? How would it have been different?
- How have we progressed together so far?

- What made you feel trusting (e.g., clear communication, positive encouragement, etc.)?
- What made you feel less trusting (e.g., laughing/joking, lack of communication, etc.)?
- What can you personally do to help increase trust in the group?
- How does what you're doing in the SELA lessons relate to the rest of your life?

Facilitation Tips

The purpose of having students discuss in pairs is so that they can get "deeper" into the conversations. Reporting back to the large group is not necessary. You can "spot check" conversations by floating between pairs to keep students "on topic."

Lesson 7

Trust

Trust Sequence III

ACTIVITIES ⚽	MATERIALS ✍
1. Hog Call (10 minutes) 2. Trust Wave (15 minutes) 3. Trust Run (15 minutes) 4. Debrief: Woofs and Wags (5 minutes)	• Blindfolds (one per student)

---

1. HOG CALL (10 MINUTES)

Objective: For student pairs to find each other while blindfolded using call and response.
Setup: Find a large open area, like a gym or a field. Have students get into pairs.
Framing: Say to students: "We need to continue to support each other throughout our time together. In this activity, you will all be blindfolded and will need to pay attention to safety and to each other in order to be successful. Remember, bumpers up."

1. Ask each pair to pick a pair of words that relates to activities from SELA (e.g., Full/Value, Trust/Lean, and Comfort/Zone). Once each partner group has selected two words, have each individual within their pair select their half phrase (call and response).
2. Ask students to share their words with the group to make sure no two pairs are alike.
3. Tell students that they will be split up and that they must all find their partners without using their sense of sight. They can only use the word they selected. Of course, this will involve lots of noise while players shout out their words and try to listen for their partner.
4. Explain that everyone will have eyes closed or be wearing a blindfold and that your job is to make sure no one runs into a wall or barrier.
5. Everyone closes their eyes or puts on their blindfold.
6. Split the pairs up and spread the students out randomly around the designated area.
7. On a signal, they start calling their part of the two-word phrase.
8. When partners find each other, they should step to the side and silently wait for others.
9. Continue until all partners are reunited.

Safety Check
Remind everyone to move slowly and keep their "bumpers up."

2. TRUST WAVE (15 MINUTES)

Objective: To experiment with physical/emotional risk and distinguish between perceived and actual risk.

Setup: Ask the class to form two lines that face each other. The distance between the two lines should be wide enough for opposing players to stand wrist to wrist if they were to extend their arms out in front of them.

Framing: Say to students: "Have you ever faced a challenge that was scary for you 'head on' rather than shying away? This activity gives you a chance to go head on into something that may appear scary. One person—the 'runner'—is given an opportunity to walk, jog, or run all the way down between these two lines. Each person in line will have their arms stretched out in front of them. Just before the 'runner' hits the arms, they are moved up and out of the way. Each participant will select his or her own level of challenge in this activity."

1. Select a volunteer to be a runner. This player should start about 10 to 15 feet from the head of the two lines. Establish a communication system like the one used in Trust Leans. The runner yells, "Ready?" and does not proceed until the group responds, "Ready."
2. The runner, using whatever pace is comfortable, approaches the lines maintaining the same speed throughout the run or walk. The spotters (all of the people in the two lines) are positioned with their arms outstretched, heads turned toward the runner. As the runner approaches them, and just before it is too late, each pair of spotters raises their arms up so that the runner passes untouched. This motion looks like a giant wave as it passes down the double line.
3. Allow the runner a second turn to increase his/her speed if they would like.
4. Allow any other student who would like to be the runner to do so.

Safety Check
Make sure that each runner starts far enough away for the group to be able to judge the runner's speed.
Use clear commands.
Use even ground.

Facilitation Tips
The activity looks easier than it is for the runner!

Optional Questions:

• Were you able to trust that the spotters would move in time? Why?
• Were you able to go faster on your second attempt? Why?
• What was the perceived risk versus the actual risk in this activity?

3. TRUST RUN (15 MINUTES)

Objective: To differentiate between emotional and physical risk.

Setup: You need a large space for this activity, about the size of a sports field. This is best done outdoors, but it can be done in a smaller indoor space. Ask students to stand in a fan or large funnel at the end of the Trust Run area.

Framing: Say to students: "You experienced a certain level of risk in the previous activity. This one will give you a chance to increase the perception of risk."

1. One by one, students will be given the opportunity to run from one end of the field or gymnasium to the other.
2. That student can move at whatever speed she/he would like; the faster the run, the greater the challenge.
3. The runner will be blindfolded.
4. The remainder of the class spreads out in a funnel at the end of the run. This funnel prevents the runner from going "out of bounds" or running too far astray.
5. Classmates are to verbally alert the runner if she is about to run into them, telling her to stop!
6. If the runner gets to the end of the funnel, spotters are to yell "Stop!" before the runner makes contact with them.

Safety Check

The field needs to be free of any obstacles, and the ground must be even and free of any holes.
Make sure the class, all acting as spotters, stays alert.
Students may choose to close their eyes instead of using a blindfold.
Many students, when blindfolded, will run in a crooked line, so be sure to have the spotters in a funnel to catch stray runners.

Facilitation Tips
Optional Questions:

* Did you respect your own comfort zone?
* What type of risk did you take in this activity, physical, emotional, or both?
* Is one type of risk harder or easier for you in other activities outside of class?

4. DEBRIEF: WOOFS AND WAGS (5 MINUTES)

1. Remind students when they portrayed animals earlier in the lesson. Say to students: "If we can, imagine today's lesson from the eyes of a puppy."
2. Ask each student to briefly share a "woof" (something that they want to bring attention to that happened during today's lesson in the group or for themselves) and a "wag" (something they want to celebrate).
3. If a student wants to pass, come back to them at the end.

Lesson 8

Goal Setting

Kaizen: The Art of Continual Improvement

ACTIVITIES ⚽

1. Moonball (10 minutes)
2. On Target (30 minutes)
3. Debrief: Efficiency/Effectiveness Odometer (5 minutes)

MATERIALS ✍

• One beach ball
• Three color-coded buckets
• Three sets of 10 balls (matched colors to buckets)
• Three On Target instruction sheets (copy from Appendix C)
• Long rope (as boundary marker)
• Efficiency and Effectiveness odometers (copy from Appendix B)
• Two pens

---

1. MOONBALL (10 MINUTES)

Objective: For the group to keep a beach ball aloft for the highest number of consecutive hits.

Framing: Say to students: "The Japanese have a concept of continual improvement called Kaizen. In this activity, you will practice Kaizen by improving your score while performing a simple task multiple times."

Setup: Clear a large open space in a room with very high ceiling or outside.

1. Students will have three tries to continuously improve their score. Each "try" consists of a cycle made up of one minute of planning and two minutes of implementation of the plan.
2. The "score" consists of the total number of "legal" hits made during each implementation cycle.
3. "Legal" hits consist of the following:
   • Only volleyball-type touches are allowed (you cannot hold or pass or kick, etc., a ball).
   • Only hands can touch the ball.
   • No person can hit a ball more than once at a time.

- No person can hit the ball a second time until everyone else on the team has hit it once.
- Heroic dives or other desperate measures are not allowed.

4. If the ball touches the ground, touches a body part other than the hands, or if it is touched out of turn, the score for legal hits immediately returns to zero. Of course, if the team still has time on the two-minute implementation clock, it can immediately start again to use the remaining time and try to increase the score.

Safety Check
Be sure that the ground area is level and clear of obstacles as people's attention will be "up."

Facilitation Tips
The secret to facilitator success with this activity is to *keep it moving* and not to allow any extra time during or between these three cycles. It is also important to be clear during the briefing that the only acceptable touch of the ball is a volleyball type "hit."

2. ON TARGET (30 MINUTES)

Objective: To get as many balls as possible into the buckets.
Setup: Clear a large space and set up the boundary line, buckets, and balls as shown below:

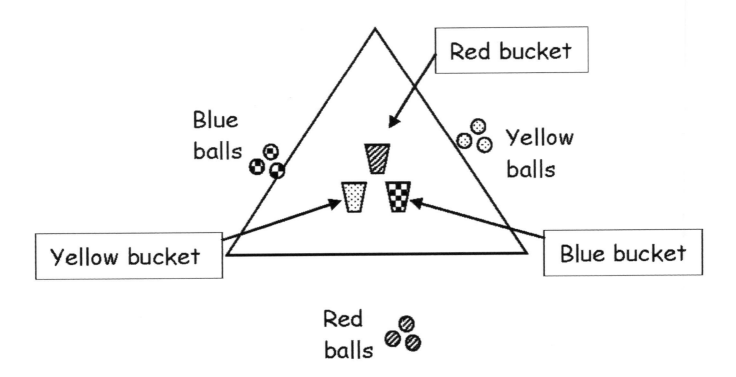

Divide the students into three even groups and have them stand on one side of the triangle.
Framing: Say to students: "In this activity, you get another chance to apply the Kaizen principle you learned from the previous activity. Your team's goal is to get the most amount of points."

The game consists of four rounds:

Round 1: After people and equipment are in place, explain that in one minute they will need to send a representative to meet with the facilitator. Share a copy of the rules (Appendix C) with the representatives, who must explain this to their small group. Explain that the representatives will have two minutes to communicate the goal and rules of the activity to their group and formulate a plan. They will have 90 seconds to achieve their goal. The facilitator will indicate the aforementioned starting and ending times. The rules may be posted or handed to the representatives. At the end of the round, ask the representatives to count the balls in the buckets. Each correct ball in the corresponding bucket equals one point. Post the results, including a total cumulative score, on a newsprint or whiteboard.

Round 2: The representatives meet with the facilitator. Explain that they have three minutes to formulate a strategy with their groups and 90 seconds to execute it. The goal for this round is to at least double their previous score. (If the groups did not score, the goal is to get one or more). The same rules apply. At the end of the round, representatives report their results to the facilitator, who will post them and announce the cumulative score.

Round 3: Repeat directions as described in Round 2.

Round 4: Same as above, plus the goal is to earn as many points as possible. Same rules apply. If they are already collaborating between sides, you might ask them to alter their approach.

Safety Check
Remind students to be mindful of others when throwing the balls.

Facilitation Tips
If students make the shift from viewing the "team" as solely comprised of their small group to being comprised of all the students playing the game, their scores will be higher.

3. DEBRIEF: EFFICIENCY/EFFECTIVENESS ODOMETER (5 MINUTES)

Setup: Photocopy the odometers (Appendix B), one for efficiency and one for effectiveness. Use two pens as dials.

1. Facilitator presents the odometers. You may wish to provide the following definitions for each word.
   - Efficiency: the ability of the group to complete a task in a timely manner with minimal off-task conversations.
   - Effectiveness: the outcome of the process. Was the job accomplished successfully, correctly, and without mistakes?
2. Group members are then asked to place each dial in the position that reflects their perception of the group's performance in both areas during Moonball and On Target. Allow time for discussion.

Lesson 9

Communication
Effective Communication Principles

ACTIVITIES ✪	MATERIALS ✍
1. Elevator Air (10 minutes) 2. Communication Breakdown (25 minutes) 3. Debrief: Nuggets (10 minutes)	• Four hula hoops • Four plush toys, rubber chickens, or other oddities • Long rope • Blindfolds (one for every group of three) • Flip chart paper • Assorted colored markers

1. ELEVATOR AIR (10 MINUTES)

Objective: To move across the circle in a variety of different ways creating connections with other team members.

Setup: Invite the group to form a circle.

Framing: Say to students: "Many of us have experienced riding in an elevator and it is often quiet and uncomfortable. We're going to create an 'elevator space' here in our classroom to see if we can change this typical impersonal situation. We will try different verbal and nonverbal behaviors to see how they affect group mood and energy."

During this activity the group will be asked to move across the circle a few different times.

1. For the first crossing, ask the group to visually select an area on the opposite side of the circle from where they are standing. They will move to this space during this first round. During this round, invite the group to imagine they are on an elevator in which they will cross the circle without making any eye contact. Remind them to be mindful of one another as they come toward the center of the circle.

2. For the second crossing, follow the same guidelines as above; however, this time each person should give a short head nod or other nonverbal response, acknowledging at least three of their group members.

3. During the third crossing, each student needs to shake hands with at least three other group members.

4. By the fourth crossing, the group will be asked to think about how they might react at the end of the school year. Invite them to imagine saying good-bye to their wonderful team members at the end of the year. It might be helpful to demonstrate a warm good-bye; this could look like a high five, a pat on the back, or a hug.

Safety Check

Remind the students to be careful as they cross the circle. Many people will be converging on the middle. This is a walking-only activity.

Facilitation Tips

Please note that some people may be uncomfortable hugging during the final circle crossing. It is important to model a variety of warm and friendly greetings.

Optional Questions:

- Which circle crossing felt the most comfortable?
- Which felt the least comfortable?
- What would our group be like if we spent our entire time together not making any eye contact?
- On which elevator level would you like our team to be on during our time together?

2. COMMUNICATION BREAKDOWN (25 MINUTES)

Objective: For groups to work together as a team to place their mystery object into the appropriate hula hoop with significant limitations to each person's role.

Setup: Set up a start line at one end of a clear, open area. Divide the students into groups of three. If there is an odd number, a fourth participant can act as an observer of the process.

Framing: Say to students: "Your small group will have to transport an unknown object to an unknown location in the room. You will each have different capacities, and you will need to rely on each other and on good, clear communication to achieve the task."

1. Explain the following individual roles. In each team there is:
   - one person who can see but cannot speak or move around (i.e., walk or move from their initial spot)
   - one person who can speak but cannot see or move around (i.e., walk or move from their initial spot)
   - one person who can move but cannot see or speak
2. Participants may choose the role they feel most comfortable with, but all three roles must be covered.
3. Before the task begins, the group has up to 10 minutes to plan their strategy and devise their communication plan. Remind students that they should be thinking about how the students who cannot speak might communicate.

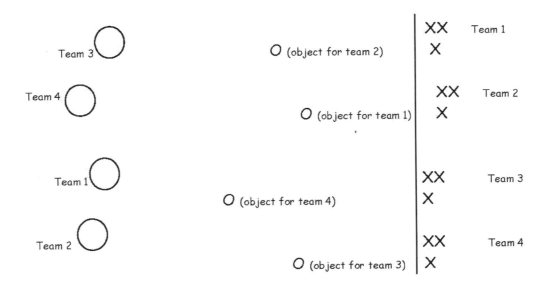

4. Once students have chosen their roles and the Speaker and Mover are blindfolded, set up the hula hoops and objects (rubber chickens, plush toys, etc.) as shown in the figure above.

5. Set out hula hoops on the other end of the open area. Hula hoops can be set out in a random arrangement. Teams may be attaining an object and placing it in a hula hoop that is *not* necessarily in a straight line in front of their group.

6. Once the props are arranged, visually point out each group's object and hula hoop to the sighted person. Check understanding with a "thumbs up."

7. Once a team of three has successfully completed the task, group members may remove their blindfolds and watch others complete the activity in silence.

8. Briefly discuss the following questions with the students:
   - How did your team develop a strategy to communicate together? What was your strategy?
   - What would occur if one of these players was removed from the system or team?

Safety Check

Be sure the game area is free from obstacles.

Students who can move but cannot see or speak should be monitored (by the facilitator) and made aware that they should move slowly ("bumpers up") to help prevent injuries (tripping or bumping into others).

Facilitation Tips

This activity can be frustrating for students. Depending on the group and their development, it may be appropriate to offer them a 60-second reprieve during the task phase to brainstorm additional communication strategies. In this case, be sure that they are behind the line and remain facing away from the resources; you may wish to keep the talker and mover blindfolded.

3. DEBRIEF: NUGGETS (10 MINUTES)

Objective: To identify effective communication principles and strategies.

Setup: Hand out a piece of flip chart paper and markers to each small Communication Breakdown group.

Framing: Say to students: "In your small groups, you will try to find 'nuggets' of effective and ineffective communication."

1. Ask students to split their pages as shown in the figure below:

Effective Communication		Ineffective Communication	
Looks like…	Sounds like…	Looks like…	Sounds like…

2. Have groups populate each column. As in any brainstorm, group members do not have to agree to write something down. Additionally, allow for contradictions that can arise for words that show up in *both* Effective and Ineffective columns.
3. Ask groups to report out and discuss how these communication strategies and principles play out for students in school and at home.

Lesson 10

Communication
Expressing Emotions

ACTIVITIES ☉	MATERIALS ✍
1. Creating a Feelings Chart (10 minutes) 2. Emotion Charades (15 minutes) 3. Balloon Trolleys (15 minutes) 4. Debrief: Small Group Questions (5 minutes)	• Flip chart paper • 40+ index cards • Balloons (one per student) • Long rope • Masking tape • Permanent markers for balloons • Feelings Chart (copy from Appendix D)

1. CREATING A FEELINGS CHART (10 MINUTES)

Objective: To identify emotion and feeling words.

Setup: Prepare a piece of flip chart paper or two by labeling different areas of the paper with each letter of the alphabet. Your students will be taping index cards with a feelings word on them under the corresponding first letter to alphabetize the words.

Framing: Say to students: "It can be hard to tell people what you are feeling. Sometimes we just don't have the words. Together we are going to start a chart to help us find the right words."

1. Ask your students to brainstorm words that describe feelings.
2. Ask for a volunteer or two to write each word on a separate index card.
3. When they have at least 15 words, ask them to tape each index card under the appropriate letter on the flip chart paper so they alphabetize the words.
4. Expand the chart by reading the following sentences for the students to finish. New words should be written on index cards.
   • When I make a mistake, I feel _____.
   • When I do a good job, I feel _____.
   • When I help someone and they say, "Thanks," I feel _____.
   • When someone calls me a name, I feel _____.
   • When my friend gets a brand new iPod and I don't have one, I feel _____.

- When someone won't share with me, I feel _____.
- When I help someone else, I feel _____.
- When someone smiles at me, I feel _____.
- When someone surprises me with a gift, I feel _____.

5. Again, ask your students to alphabetize these words.
6. Separate your students into three equal or roughly equal groups.
7. Give each small group one or more of the starting letters for which students currently have no words.
8. Challenge each group to come up with three or more new words using one or more of their starting letters. Let them know that they need to be words that describe a feeling and that they need to be prepared to define this word and use it in a sentence.
9. As groups report out, they should post new words written on index cards on the flip chart paper in alphabetical order.

Facilitation Tips

There is no right or wrong answer, just how students feel. However, one should weed out any inappropriate or antisocial responses. In the Appendix D, a list of feelings has been provided that can be used for supplementing students' responses.

Use the newly created index cards in the next activity and keep them on hand for future check-ins and/or debriefs.

2. EMOTION CHARADES (15 MINUTES)

Objective: To act out a feeling and have other students guess the representation.
Setup: Divide the class into groups of four to six.
Framing: Say to students: "We are going to play charades. Only in this game we will be guessing feeling and emotion words."

1. Give each group a stack of feeling index cards set face down.
2. Students take turns choosing a card and acting it out for their group members to guess. When the feeling is guessed, another person takes a turn.
3. If the group is having a hard time guessing the feeling, the person doing the charade can show them the card and pick a new one or ask someone in their group for help.
4. Perform two to three rounds of three minutes each.
5. Between rounds, check in with the groups about the different emotions. Were they easy to act out? Which ones were harder to act out (or unknown)?

Facilitation Tips

This activity can easily become competitive, which each small group trying to get more cards than the next. Obviously, this detracts from the true focus of the activity, which is to practice and learn about feelings. It is possible to minimize the competitive nature of the activity by publicly stating that each group has a different set of cards and deemphasizing the competition. Of course, if competition becomes a factor in this activity, it is a topic that is worth processing.

3. BALLOON TROLLEYS (15 MINUTES)

Objective: To reflect on how unexpressed emotions in relationships can lead to regret, disappointment, or miscommunication.

Setup: Set up a curvy path throughout your space. Make turns challenging but not too tight as students will have to pass through the path while connected to one another. You can outline this path with masking tape, activity ropes, or boundary markers.

Framing: Say to students: "We've all experienced regret and disappointment from not sharing our feelings. You leave a situation and think, 'I should've said _____' to so and so. I'd like you to think of one of these moments and the emotion or feeling that you chose not to express at that time. Keep it to yourself for now."

1. Pass one balloon to each student and ask them to blow up the balloons and tie them off. Assist students as needed.
2. Ask each student to label their balloon with permanent marker with the emotion they identified. Remind them that they won't need to share the relationship or the incident, but they will need to share the emotion.
3. Ask students to form a line with group members, standing front to back, like a trolley. Have each student place a balloon between him- or herself and the person in front of them.
4. The person at the front of the line will simply hold his or her balloon out in front.
5. Explain that they can only use each other's pressure to support the balloons—no hands, arms, or feet.
6. Explain that the challenge is to move the entire group through the path while staying connected to one another and not allowing any of the balloons to hit the floor.
7. Have students place their hands on the shoulders of the person in front of them.
8. If a balloon hits the floor, the group should stop and retrieve the balloon, and the student who was in the front of the line should move to the end, putting his or her balloon between him- or herself and the person in front of them. The group can then carry on from where they lost the balloon.
9. Have all your students form one large circle when they finish the circuit.

Safety Check

Keep an eye out for responses and comments regarding appropriate touching.

Divide the group into smaller groups if you are concerned with the students' abilities to manage physical closeness. You can also place the balloons between the students as they stand side by side, if that is more manageable. Also offer the option for students to be spotters if they are uncomfortable with the given body positions.

Facilitation Tips

If you have the time and you feel your students would be responsive, you could explore the symbolism of not being able to use your hands or feet to hold up the balloon—how an unexpressed emotion really limits a relationship.

4. DEBRIEF: SMALL GROUP QUESTIONS (5 MINUTES)

1. Ask each student to share the emotion they wrote on their balloons and how expressing their emotions would have changed the situation or the relationship.
2. If students wish to pass, come back to them at the end.
3. Finish the activity by letting them pop their balloons. If that would be too loud to do indoors, pass around scissors. After a student shares, they can cut their balloon right at the knot.

Lesson 11

Communication
Giving and Receiving Feedback

ACTIVITIES ⚽

1. Caught Ya Peekin' (5 minutes)
2. Lego Statue (35 minutes)
3. Debrief: Plus/Delta (5 minutes)

MATERIALS ✎

- Legos

---

1. CAUGHT YA PEEKIN' (5 MINUTES)

Objective: A quick warm-up game where students catch each other peeking.

Setup: Have students form a circle (either sitting or standing) where everyone can see everyone else.

Framing: Say to students: "You know how some people say, 'It's only breaking the rules if you get caught.' Well, usually that's not a good way to approach problems in life. *But*, in this game, not getting caught is the whole point!"

1. Have all students close their eyes.
2. The object of the game is for each player to open their eyes in an attempt to catch another person with their eyes open as well. Sometimes these two will spy each other at the same time, or one may catch the other looking in another direction.
3. When a person observes another with their eyes open, they are entitled to call out loudly, "Caught ya peekin'," and then call that person's name (e.g., "Caught ya peekin', José").
4. If two people spy each other at the same moment, whoever calls out first and correctly identifies the other's name wins the duel.
5. When a person is caught, have them place their hands on the top of their heads to make it clear to all those who are still playing that they are out of the game and are entitled to have their eyes open to enjoy the rest of the game.
6. Variation: To encourage lots of peeking and have the game last a little longer, grant each student three lives.

2. LEGO STATUE (35 MINUTES)

Objective: To make an exact replica of an existing Lego statue.

Setup: Using basic building blocks (e.g., Legos), build a statue comprised of 30 to 40 pieces ahead of time. Do not let students see this, and place it out of sight from the group (e.g., in the hallway, under a towel). This will be the model that students attempt to replicate. Each sub-group's staging area will require the exact same pieces used in the statue and should be about 15 feet away and out of sight of the model.

1. Split the group into two subgroups of six.
2. Each subgroup should designate two students to be the builders for the entire activity.
3. Everyone else will pair up and become the architects.
4. One pair of students (architects only) at a time may leave the staging area to look at the model. The model may not be touched or picked up at any time. The students viewing the model may not take written notes or draw the model.
5. Each pair of architects is allowed one minute to view the model.
6. After viewing the model, the pair of architects returns to the builder's table and has one minute to give verbal-only direction to the builders.
7. After the reporting minute is up, the next pair of architects may then go to the viewing table.
8. After the initial student pairs have both seen and reported on the model, they may switch partners with each other (i.e., form new architect pairs). This partner swapping may continue throughout the activity.
9. The group has five minutes to plan their strategy before any viewing or building takes place.
10. At any time during the process, either builders or architects may call a time-out to engage in a planning session.
11. The group has 30 minutes from the time they start planning to the end of the activity.
12. When the time is up, have groups compare their reproductions to the model.

Facilitation Tips

The model should have a variety of colors and shapes and should be organized in a random fashion. You may wish to have the subgroup's staging areas separate (if you want to promote independence) or near each other (if you want to promote, or allow, collaboration).

Depending on the group, you may choose to switch the builders with the architects midway through the activity (as in instruction #8 above).

To make the activity more difficult, include extra pieces as distracters.

Optional Questions:

Have everyone look at the original Lego statue and compare it to the one they built.

• Describe what happened in the activity.
• What was the most successful part for you?
• What was the most challenging part?

3. DEBRIEF: PLUS/DELTA (5 MINUTES)

Objective: To have students give and receive feedback to each other about their participation in the last activity.

Setup: Have the students sit in their subgroups for this debrief.

Framing: Say to students: "The ability to receive feedback is essential to self-awareness. Good feedback can be seen as a gift to help someone develop." Explain the following four reminders in giving feedback: Concise, Concrete, Caring, and Constructive.

1. Round 1: Ask each student to assess themselves and share their self-feedback (one specific thing that they thought they did well [plus] in the previous activity and one thing they could have improved on [delta]) with the group.
2. Round 2: Ask each student to give feedback (one plus, one delta) to the person to their left.
3. Round 3: Ask each student to give feedback (one plus, one delta) to the person to their right.

Problem Solving
Individual Contributions to Group Success

ACTIVITIES ⚽

1. Salt and Pepper (5 minutes)
2. Turnstile (10 minutes)
3. 1, 2, 3 = 20 (25 minutes)
4. Debrief: Pass the Knot (5 minutes)

MATERIALS ✍

• Long skipping rope

---

1. SALT AND PEPPER (5 MINUTES)

Objective: A fun warm-up activity.

Setup: Clear a space in the classroom and lay the rope down the middle. Ask students to stand on one side of the line.

Framing: Say to students: "This is a fun activity to get us warmed up and test our reaction time."

1. Designate one side of the line as "salt" and the other as "pepper."
2. It's pretty simple from here. You call out "salt" or "pepper," and the group members must jump to the correct side or remain on the side which represents the call. It sounds something like this: "salt . . . pepper . . . salt . . . salt . . ."
3. If someone jumps when they shouldn't, or is too slow in their jumping, they are "out of the game." You can also give students a number of "lives" before they are eliminated.
4. Variation: For each mistake, students get a point, with the intention of having the least amount of points at the end of the game, or you can also play the game just for fun!

Safety Check

Students should have enough space in front of and behind them so as not to hit one another while jumping.

Facilitation Tips

When you are completely unpredictable—both in terms of pace and timing—the suspense is palpable. Misleading can be fun: "Sssssspepper."

2. TURNSTILE (10 MINUTES)

Objective: To get everyone through the turning rope.

Setup: Select an additional rope turner to assist you. Ask the rest of the class to stand on one side of the jump rope.

Framing: Say to students: "This activity requires the entire class to participate both in solving the problem and in implementing the solution. The task is simple: *Everyone* must get through the turning rope."

Rules are:

1. One person at a time in the rope-jumping area.
2. Each player must move through the turning rope. No diving or tumbling though the rope.
3. No missing a beat (no having the rope turn without someone in).
4. If anyone misses, the entire group begins again.
5. The initiative continues until the entire class has gone through the rope. Be sure to rotate the additional rope turner out so they jump as well.

Safety Check

If a player trips or catches on the rope, the rope turners should stop turning to avoid injury. Diving through the rope is not allowed!

Facilitation Tips

Allow students to run through under the rope without jumping.

3. 1, 2, 3 = 20 (25 minutes)

Objective: The task is similar to turnstile, but the students need to solve the riddle "1, 2, 3 = 20" to figure out how to move through the rope.

Setup: Same as for Turnstile.

Framing: Say to students: "Your goal is to get the entire class to the other side of this turning rope. The only way to achieve the goal is to pass through the turning rope. The catch is you can only move through the rope using the pattern in the following riddle: 1, 2, 3 = 20. Trial and error are the only way to solve it. Try everyone's ideas!"

1. Start turning the rope. The riddle starts (see Solution below) once the first student passes through.
2. The rope will continue turning as long as the group's actions are correct.
3. The rope will immediately stop turning as soon as the group does anything that is incorrect.
4. The only way to solve the riddle is to physically enter the rope. The solution will be found if the group focuses on the number of people who pass through the rope. (The exact solution is listed at Facilitation Tips.)

5. Students will receive feedback in the following ways: Whenever the rope stops turning, you will know that you are solving the riddle incorrectly, and the class should return to the starting place/position and begin again. If you pay close attention to the moment when the rope stops turning and what the group was doing just prior to the rope stopping, you will gather important information that will assist you in solving the riddle.
6. When the rope stops, the group should stop working and analyze what happened. The group should focus on what they are doing to discover what actions are solving the riddle and what actions cause the rope to stop.

Safety Check

Drop the rope when someone trips or gets caught up in the turnstile and let the group know this was for safety, not because they were incorrect in solving the riddle.
Be aware of the footwear of your group. Flip-flops, sandals, or other loose-fitting types of foot-wear could lead to a twisted ankle.

Facilitation Tips

Allow people to run through the rope.
It is critical to count out loud to your group when they are on the right track, for example if they have one person go through, shout out "one." If they follow that with two, shout "two." If they follow that with three, shout out "three," and so on.

Solution:

One person passes through the rope, then two people, then three people; this pattern (1, 2, 3) is then repeated until the rope has turned a total of 20 rotations (i.e., 1, 2, 3, 1, 2, 3, 1, 2, 3, 1 . . .). Students will have to recycle group members back to the starting side of the rope to achieve the solution. They should come around the sides.

4. DEBRIEF: PASS THE KNOT (5 MINUTES)

Objective: To reflect on behaviors that helped/hurt the group to solve the problem.
Setup: Tie two ends of rope together to form into a circle. Use any knot that will hold. Have the group stand in a circle loosely holding the knotted rope.
Framing: Say to students: "As the knot in the rope is passed to you, please share one behavior that helped your group to solve the initiative and one behavior that hurt your ability to solve the initiative today. Once you have shared, pass the knot to your left to the next person."

1. Have students share responses to the question above and then pass the knot when they are finished.
2. If a student wants to "pass," you can come back to them at the end.

Safety Check

Do not allow students to tug on the rope or hold firmly, as they could get rope burn.

Lesson 13

Problem Solving
Introduce ABCDE Model

ACTIVITIES ⚽	MATERIALS ✍
1. Silent Lineup (10 minutes) 2. Warp Speed (15 minutes) 3. Star Wars (15 minutes) 4. Debrief: Continuum (5 minutes)	• Fleece ball or other soft object to throw (Nerf ball or stuffed animal) • Star Wars kit • Warp Speed Rule Sheet (copy from Appendix E) • ABCDE Problem-Solving Model—one per student (copy from Appendix F)

1. SILENT LINEUP (10 MINUTES)

Objective: To work together as a team to successfully get into a single file line in a specific order.
Setup: Have students circle up.

1. Explain to students that, in a moment, you will ask them to order themselves in a particular way. They will not be able to speak or write and must find another way to communicate.
2. Once you give the directive, enforce the no-talking rule.
3. Have students line up in two or three different orders.
4. Debrief: Ask students how they arrived at a decision when not able to speak or write.

Facilitation Tips
Lineup suggestions: Height, number of letters in your first name, birthday, how far you travel to school.

2. WARP SPEED (15 MINUTES)

Objective: To complete this problem-solving activity in the fastest time possible and adhere to all of the rules.

Setup: Arrange your group in a circle. Do not include yourself, as you will be keeping time.

Framing: In this activity, students will use problem-solving and listening skills to work together to accomplish the task. It is generally sufficient to tell the group that they will need to work together to solve a problem, while increasing the speed with which they accomplish the task.

1. Set up a new throwing pattern in the group using the same guidelines as for Group Juggle (see Lesson 3). Students do not need to use each other's names or the Full Value Concepts for this activity.
2. Hand out a photocopy of the accompanying Rules Sheet (Appendix E) and have students read them.
3. Have students go through an initial speed attempt and note their time.
4. After an initial time is established, ask them to see if they can reduce that time by working together as a group.
5. The next couple of sequenced attempts usually show more cooperation and teamwork, and completion time drops appreciably. If the first time is 50 seconds, considering their great teamwork, ask them to cut it in half. Allow a couple of minutes for brainstorming. If there are too many ideas, suggest that they try one idea at a time.

Facilitation Tips

Allow the group to try many different options, including breaking out of the circle formation. If students ask questions, redirect them to the Rules Sheet. Avoid interpreting rules for the students.

3. STAR WARS (15 MINUTES)

Objective: To have students use a formal problem-solving strategy and think outside the box.

Setup: Have students stand in a circle.

Framing: Introduce and describe the ABCDE model of problem solving (Appendix F). Make connections to how students solved the previous initiative. Encourage students to keep this tool in mind as they approach the next problem.

1. Have each student take a looped rope, place it on the floor, and stand in the loop.
2. Tell the students: "There is only one rule in this activity: both feet have to be inside the circle. When I say 'switch,' you need to walk to a different loop and put both feet inside the circle. I may call 'quality control,' which means that you look at your feet and those around you to make sure everyone is following the rule: both feet inside the circle."
3. After you have had the group do two or three switches, remove one or two loops. Keep removing loops until you are down to the eight-foot extra-large loop that will not allow the group to stand inside the circle.
4. The group needs to figure out a way to have everyone's feet within the circle. As a facilitator, you can only go back to the "both feet inside the circle" rule; do not hint at any solutions.

Safety Check
Do not allow students to get on each other's shoulders or backs.

Facilitation Tips
The end solution once you have gotten to the last circle is for almost all of the people to sit with their feet within the circle and their bodies outside.

Small: 4 × 3'
Medium: 4 × 5'
Large: 3 × 6'
Extra Large: 1 × 8'

4. DEBRIEF: CONTINUUM (5 MINUTES)

Objective: To help students quickly reflect on their adherence to the ABCDE model.
Framing: Say to students: "We are going to use an imaginary continuum to show how successful you think we were today."

Designate a continuum of success across the room. The ends should represent efforts that were "Very Poor" to "Excellent" (see figure below).

Ask the entire group, "How well did the group do at using the ABCDE Problem-Solving Model? Place yourself on the continuum."
Check in with individual students:

• "Why did you place yourself there? Can you give a specific example of this?"
• "What would the group need to do for you to rate it higher?"

Facilitation Tips
In addition to "Why did you place yourself there?" types of questions, you can ask paradoxical questions. For example, to high-rating students, you can ask what would help increase their score even more, and to low-rating students, you can ask what allowed them to be a 3/10 instead of a 0/10 (i.e., seeking the positive in a low-rated evaluation).

Additional Optional Questions:

• Who came up with the final idea?
• How did you come up with that idea?

- What were you all thinking when I said "both feet in the circle"?
- This activity is all about thinking outside of the box. What does that mean? Give me an example of when you thought outside of the box at school.
- How do you think that concept will help you in school?

Lesson 14

Problem Solving
Applying the ABCDE Model

ACTIVITIES ⚽

1. RPS World Championship (5 minutes)
2. Group Blackjack (10 minutes)
3. Change Up (20 minutes)
4. Debrief: Deck of Cards (10 minutes)

MATERIALS ✍

• One deck of playing cards

---

1. RPS WORLD CHAMPIONSHIP (5 MINUTES)

Objective: To win the group rock-paper-scissor (RPS) championship or actively support the winners if you lose your turn.

Framing: Explain to students the rules of rock-paper-scissors.

1. Students individually challenge each other to a game of rock-paper-scissors.
2. The student who loses becomes the winner's most ardent fan, applauding and cheering for the winner.
3. The winner (along with their supporting fans) goes on to challenge another student (who may also have their own support fans).
4. The losing student and *all* their fans become supporters of the *new* winner. In this way, the winners' fan base/entourage grows exponentially.
5. Repeat this process until there is one "world champion" with everybody else in the class cheering for them.

2. GROUP BLACKJACK (10 MINUTES)

Objective: To work together as a team to successfully get into groups with cards totaling 19, 20, or 21.

Setup: Have students circle up.

Framing: Say to students: "Here are some simple blackjack rules in case you are unfamiliar with the game: Aces equal a value of 1 or 11. Jack, queen, and king cards equal a value of 10. All other number cards are face value."

1. Give each participant a card and ask them not to look at it. (If someone peeks at their card, have them trade cards with their neighbor.)
2. Inform the group that this is a silent activity and they may not use their voices for the duration of the activity.
3. Ask them to place their card to their forehead so it is visible to the rest of their team.
4. Instruct them to play blackjack as a large group. Using addition only, each participant must be included in a "hand" that equals a combined value of 19, 20, or 21.

Facilitation Tips

Be sure to deal in a few aces to make this possible. The inclusion of one "joker" will also make the initiative easier.

When given a range of 19, 20, and 21, group members should be able to include everyone in the group no matter how many participants you have.

3. CHANGE UP (20 MINUTES)

Objective: To order the group as quickly as possible based on "changing" parameters.

Setup: Use only one suit for Challenge 1. Use a second suit and have it ready for a second challenge (one red and one black).

Framing: Say to students: "Your group will be given a challenge. You will be given three minutes to plan based on the ABCDE model. After planning, your group will attempt the challenge. The group will then be given another three minutes to evaluate and plan the second round. Once the second round is accomplished, the second challenge will be given to the group. The process will begin again."

1. Hand out one card per student (only draw from one suit). Instruct students that they are not allowed to look at their card.
2. Say to students: "Challenge 1: Turn your cards over and place it on your forehead. Now line yourselves up in numerical order from smallest to largest card number. Aces are low, kings are high."
3. Time the students for the first round and post the time on the board. Allow time for evaluation and planning. Have the students shuffle the cards by exchanging cards with at least three people. Complete a few rounds to improve the time score.
4. Say to students: "Challenge 2: Turn your cards over. Line yourselves up in numerical order by suit in two lines—one red, one black." Repeat rounds as above.

4. DEBRIEF: DECK OF CARDS (10 MINUTES)

Objective: To reflect on the group's problem-solving process.
Setup: Have students circle up and shuffle the entire deck of cards.
Framing: Say to students: "We're each going to draw a card and, depending on the suit, we'll answer a different question about our activities."

1. Have students each draw a card.
2. Ask participants to share a thought based on the suit they draw:
   - Hearts: What did you feel?
   - Spades: What were some of the ideas you "dug up"?
   - Clubs: What new ideas grew during this activity?
   - Diamonds: What is a gem (object of value) that you saw?
3. Collect cards. Start over at 1 one with fresh cards for students to answer for a second time, but this time ask how they think the group has done throughout the entire SELA program to date.

Facilitation Tips
Optional Questions:

- What strategies or techniques did you use in this activity that you have developed from previous activities?
- What solutions did you come up with from the first challenge that worked well for the other challenges?
- What part of the ABCDE model worked well for this group? Which part needs more work to be effective?

Lesson 15

Reflection

Review Semester and Celebrate Highlights

ACTIVITIES ☺	MATERIALS ✍
1. Who Am I? (10 minutes) 2. Virtual Slide Show (20 minutes) 3. Debrief: Did Ya? (15 minutes)	• SELA Skills written on poster board or whiteboard • SELA Skills cards (copy from Appendix G) • Scotch or masking tape

1. WHO AM I? (10 minutes)

Objective: To review the life skills that students developed during the fall SELA lessons.

Setup: Begin this lesson with an overview of the skills that were explored during the SELA program to date. Have the following written on a poster board or dry erase board:

- Self-Awareness
- Healthy Relationships
- Effective Communication
- Goal Setting
- Problem Solving
- Community Building
- Conflict Resolution
- Building Trust
- Leadership

Framing: Say to students: "It is important that we all understand these skills. We should be able not only to list them but also to describe them and, even more importantly, to identify them in others and ourselves."

1. Print one copy of SELA Skills cards (Appendix G) on stiff paper or card stock. Cut into cards so there is one card per student.

2. Ask each student to tape a card on another student's back. It is important that no one knows the card that is on their back.

3. Each student is to discover their characteristic by asking yes or no questions of others in the class. Student cannot ask the specific question "Am I 'leadership'?" until they have asked three previous exploratory questions.

4. Only one question can be asked of any one person.

5. Answers can only be "yes" or "no."

6. When the student correctly identifies the skill on his or her back, the card is removed.

7. The activity continues until everyone has identified his or her characteristic.

Facilitation Tips

If you have more students than SELA skills, repeat as many as appropriate to have one card per student.

2. VIRTUAL SLIDE SHOW (20 MINUTES)

Objective: To review and celebrate the highlights of the fall.

Setup: Have students sit in a semicircle looking at a blank movie screen or whiteboard (as if they are to watch a film). An imaginary screen is also fine.

Framing: Say to students: "Imagine you are going to see a slide show of some of our best moments and accomplishments this fall. Each of us will share a few slides."

1. As a facilitator, explain the operation of the clicker. Tell the group, "On the count of three, let's all make the sound that a slide projector clicker makes. One, two, three, click!" Then narrate what your image shows: "In this next slide, you'll see . . ."

2. Ask your students to think of two or three pictures they would want to present about their time in the SELA lessons.

3. When students are ready, make the clicker sound all together and go around the circle, presenting one slide at a time.

Facilitation Tips

This activity has an uncanny way of taking the spotlight away from the speaker and directs it to the slide show. It helps those who are uncomfortable with the group staring at them while they are sharing.

3. DEBRIEF: DID YA? (15 MINUTES)

Objective: To explore common reactions to the semester/curriculum.

Setup: Have your group stand in a circle. Put spot markers at the foot of each person (not including yourself). Add a final marker for yourself (which can be a different color or size), and designate that as the "question-asking spot."

Framing: Say to students: "We are going to play a variation of Have You Ever? where we can learn what folks have gotten out of the semester."

1. Ask the first Did Ya? question (to set the tone). Example, "Did ya get to know someone else in our class better than you knew them before SELA?" or "Did ya speak up during our lessons more than you would in other classes?"

2. Explain to students: "If your answer to the question is yes, then you are to move from your spot to a new spot, but not the spot next door. If your answer is no, then you are to remain on your spot. One student will end up on the question-asking spot. Once everyone is settled, that new person will ask the next question."

3. The person in the question-asking spot must move to a new spot regardless of whether he or she did or did not answer "yes" to the question. This assures a new person each time.

4. During the activity, you may ask some related follow-up questions to the students who have moved, such as "I'm curious about that. Tell me more."

5. Variation: Students can come up with their own Did Ya questions, or you can have them written out on index cards and allow the reader to ask one of the facilitator's questions.

Safety Check

Remind students to be mindful of not bumping into one another as they walk to a new spot.

Lesson 16

Regroup

Full Value Contract: Semester Review

ACTIVITIES ⚽	MATERIALS ✎
1. Gotcha FVC Review (5 minutes) 2. Stargate (30 minutes) 3. Debrief: The Being Revisited (10 minutes)	• Full Value Contract: The Being and the list of Full Value Concepts • Bungee cord loop made from quarter-inch bungee, large enough for the biggest person to fit through if bungee is moderately stretched

1. GOTCHA FVC REVIEW (5 MINUTES)

Objective: To review the group's Full Value Contract with a fun game.

Setup: Ask the class to stand in a tight circle.

Framing: Say to students: "Welcome back! We're going to play a quick fun game. We'll also use this game to remind ourselves of our Full Value Concepts."

1. Have students review their Full Value Concepts. Prompt them to consider what this might mean in the following activity (e.g., Be Here = being focused and present; Be Honest = acknowledging if your finger was caught or not).
2. Ask the students to put their right hand, palm facing up, in front of the stomach of the person to their right.
3. Next, ask them to take their left index finger and point it into the middle of the palm that is now in front of their own stomach.
4. Explain that on the count of three they have two tasks: to catch the finger in their right palm and to keep their own index finger free.
5. You should point out the simple rule of "no cupping," which involves not allowing people to cup their hands in order to have a better chance to catch the finger in their palm.
6. Count to three. Watch students have fun with catching or missing. Then tell students that if they catch someone, they can turn to them and say "Gotcha!"
7. After a few rounds, you may ask different students to count to three.

8. Variations: Change hands to left hand out in front of the person to your left, and right index finger in the palm in front of your stomach. Rather than having palms facing up, have palms start higher in the air and face down, with index finger pointing up.

Facilitation Tips
Keep this moving and fun. Once you sense the energy waning, move on to the next activity.

2. STARGATE (30 MINUTES)

Objective: To have the entire group pass through a small loop of bungee cord without touching it.
Setup: Have the group stand in a circle.
Framing: Say to students: "The goal of this activity is to get the entire class through the circle of bungee cord! This is a chance for us to explore how we will continue to support each other in taking risks. As you go through the loop, please tell the class one thing that they can do to assist you in taking other risks."

1. Each person must remain physically in contact with the rest of the group via at least one other person. The cord holder must be in contact with both the class and the cord.
2. There can be as many cord holders as you would like. However, the person going through the loop cannot touch it. If they do, the entire group starts again.
3. Each cord holder can only hold the loop with one hand.
4. Subsequent rounds can be played by asking the class to set time goals for themselves.

Safety Check
Ask the class not to stretch the cord and let it go, as it could snap and injure someone.
If the class is moving rapidly, be sure that shoulders and backs are attended to.

Facilitation Tips
Make sure the loop can accommodate the largest person in the class.

Optional Questions:

- What were the emotional and physical risks involved in this activity?
- What were the things that people asked for prior to going through the cord?
- How did the class demonstrate appropriate support during this activity? Did this support help the class be more successful? Explain.
- As a class, do you think you can give people the kind of support they need? If so, how? If not, why not?
- Talk with a partner about your individual responsibility to help maintain an environment where appropriate risks can be taken. What will be hard and easy for you to do? Share with the rest of the class.

3. DEBRIEF: THE BEING REVISITED (10 MINUTES)

Objective: To review and add to the group's Full Value Contract, The Being.

Setup: Lay out The Being and ask students to gather around it.

Framing: "We created our Being at the start of the year as a way to identify what is important to us and how we want to be together as a group. Let's take some time to review our Being to see if there are any changes we feel we need to make to it before we recommit ourselves to our norms."

1. Ask students to take a moment and read all the words and concepts they had written down on The Being.
2. Have students form groups of three and discuss:
   - Which concepts most helped them work as a group in the first half of the year?
   - Any concepts or tools that they think would help the group move forward that are not included on The Being (or that are no longer useful and should be removed).
   - Which concept they think they need to (and can) work on in the coming months?
3. Have students report back. The group should also discuss any proposed modifications to The Being and make these as required.
4. Finish the debrief with students, recommitting to uphold The Being.

Lesson 17

Goal Setting

Setting Behavioral Goals for the Semester

ACTIVITIES	MATERIALS
1. How Do You Do? (10 minutes) 2. I'm OK, You're OK Tag (10 minutes) 3. Goal Mapping (15 minutes) 4. Debrief: Gallery Walk of Goals (10 minutes)	• Goal Mapping sheets—one per student (copy from Appendix H) • Writing utensils (one per person) • String • Masking tape

1. HOW DO YOU DO? (10 MINUTES)

Objective: To experience acknowledgment from one's peers.

Setup: Have your group stand in a circle with one person in the middle.

Framing: Say to students: "It is important to acknowledge people all the time, but especially if you are going to help them achieve their goals."

1. The middle person approaches someone in the circle, looks him or her in the eyes, shakes his or her hand, and says, "How do you do?" The person who is approached answers, "Fine, thanks!" They repeat this three times.

2. After the third handshake, the pair splits, one running in one direction around the outside of the circle, the other running in the opposite direction outside the circle.

3. They will meet again about halfway around. When they do, they are to stop, shake hands, and say "How do you do?" and "Fine, thanks!" one time.

4. Next they race back to the original starting point. Whoever arrives last goes back into the middle of the circle.

5. While the runners are moving around the circle, the other students can extend their hand whenever they would like, which *requires* the runner to stop, make eye contact with them, shake hands, and say, "How do you do?" to which the runner responds, "Fine, thanks." This incorporates everyone into the activity and slows down the outside runners.

Safety Check

Ask the runners to move at a safe speed. This may be a fast walk (or heel-to-toe) if the circle is very small.

Ask students in the circle to put their hands out early enough so as not to hit runners.

Facilitation Tips
Optional Questions:

- What did it feel like to be acknowledged?
- What did it feel like to acknowledge others?

2. I'M OK, YOU'RE OK TAG (10 MINUTES)

Objective: To identify ways in which students can support each other.

Setup: You will need an open space where the group can circle up and move around.

Framing: Say to students: "One strategy for achieving our goals is to have a 'buddy' and a plan. Your friends can be sources of support during times when achieving goals might seem hard. This activity will help you to practice finding one another amid the chaos that we sometimes experience during life."

1. Ask students to find partners and form a circle inside the open space, standing next to their partners.
2. Tell the students they are going to play a fun tag activity with their partners.
3. In other words, tell them, "Just you and your partner will be chasing one another, but everyone will do that at the same time."
4. Ask the group to imagine they are at a big party with their friend and they have agreed to check in with one another every so often to make sure they are both OK.
5. Explain that this tag activity represents the party and that when you tag your partner, you say, "Are you OK?" That person says, "I'm OK," and counts to 10 while you get away.
6. Tell students that once they are tagged, their partner becomes the tagger and will chase them after they count to 10. When they find their partner, they tag that person and say, "Are you OK?" That person says, "I'm OK," counts to 10, and repeats the process.
7. Remind students that once they have answered the questions, the person who is now being chased should move away from his/her partner while that partner is counting to 10.
8. Have each partnership decide who will start as the tagger and begin.

Safety Check

Be sure the game area is big enough and clear of tripping hazards. Students should be mindful of each other and keep their "bumpers" up.

Facilitation Tips
Optional Questions:

- How did it feel to make contact (tag) with your support buddy throughout the activity?
- How can your goal buddy be helpful and be someone you seek out versus someone you run away from?
- What ways did you stay connected to your partner even when you were separated or moving away from them?
- If you really were at a party, what are some ways you could let your friends know that you are not OK?

3. GOAL MAPPING (15 MINUTES)

Objective: To describe the benefits of positive and challenging goals.
Setup: Give each student a copy of the Goal Mapping worksheet (Appendix H).
Framing: Say to students: "Sometimes when we set goals, we say the things we think we should say without really thinking about the benefits of achieving that goal. For example, students often say that they have a goal of staying focused in class, without thinking through the benefits of achieving the goals, such as getting more done, getting better grades, and earning more respect from their peers and teachers."

1. Hand out worksheets to each student.
2. Explain the following: Start with the central idea of what you desire to change. Write it in the big circle. This becomes the goal to focus on. It is the central idea.
3. Next, consider the "Benefits" from making this change.
4. Do the same with your "Abilities" to make this change. Think about what might get in the way. What are your assets that will help you make this change and overcome things that get in the way?
5. In the "Need" bubbles, describe your reasons for focusing on this goal.
6. Encourage students to add additional bubbles for any subtopic as they see fit.

4. DEBRIEF: GALLERY WALK OF GOALS (10 MINUTES)

1. Ask students to visually represent their goal (use the reverse side of the Goal Mapping sheet). They can use symbols, words, or drawings. Ask students to include one to three specific ways in which the group can support them in achieving their goal.
2. Hang up a string like a clothesline and ask students to hang up their goal sheets (use masking tape).
3. Ask students to spend time, in silence, looking at everyone's goals and reflecting on how they can support each specific goal.
4. Ask students to briefly present their goal and facilitate a short discussion on how students can provide support for each other's goals.

5. Collect student worksheets, as they will be used in Lesson 23. You may also refer students back to them throughout the semester.

Facilitation Tips
Optional Questions:

• How does this goal apply to the classroom/unit?
• Do we need to add anything to this map?

Lesson 18

Healthy Relationships
Awareness of Personal Qualities

ACTIVITIES ⚽	MATERIALS ✍
1. My Qualities (5 minutes) 2. Stepping Stones (25 minutes) 3. Debrief: Small Group Questions (15 minutes)	• Quality cards, two sets (copy from Appendix I) • Masking tape • Stepping stones (one per student) • Two short boundary lines/ropes

1. MY QUALITIES (5 MINUTES)

Objective: To identify personal qualities and strengths that students bring to the group.

Setup: Lay out the cut-out Quality cards (Appendix I) in an open area in the classroom and have students circle around them. Blank cards are provided if you want to add qualities.

Framing: Say to students: "As we have worked together this year, you have all brought different qualities and abilities to our group. In the rush of school life, it's sometimes important to take a moment and reflect on what we do well."

1. Explain to the students that, in a moment, you will ask them to pick up a quality or ability that they feel they bring to the group. Some of the cards are labeled, whereas others are blank. Blank notes can be filled in by students as necessary.

2. In small groups of two or three, have students briefly explain why they chose a particular quality.

Facilitation Tips

Make two copies of the Quality cards and cut them out ahead of time. Having two sets allows multiple students to choose the same quality (e.g., challenge). Card stock or heavier paper is optimal.

2. STEPPING STONES (25 MINUTES)

Objective: To get the entire group from one side of the "river" to the other side using the stepping stones.

Setup: Put the two boundary lines approximately 15 to 25 feet apart. Vary the distance based on student numbers and desired difficulty (wider is harder). Have each student tape their quality onto a stepping stone.

Framing: The area between the start and finish lines can be described to the students as a river to cross, the time between now and the end of the school year, etc. Be creative with a story or metaphor. Say to students: "The group must work together, using all of the words that they have written on their stepping stones, to successfully make it to the other side."

1. The students must work together to get the entire group to the other side.
2. The stepping stones must always remain in contact with the students. If a person loses contact with a stone, it will be lost.
3. If a student touches the ground or steps off a stepping stone, the entire group must start over.

Safety Check
Use caution. The stepping stones could slip on polished floors.

Facilitation Tips
If the group asks, they may practice outside the bounded area with no penalty.

When you are giving the instructions, do not dwell on the directions about being in contact with the stones. Watch carefully as the participants often lay down a stepping stone within the boundary area without keeping in contact with it. If so, pick it up without saying anything. If they ask about it, you can respond by asking them, "Which guideline did your group not follow?" After the first one, they will be more careful, but groups seem to relax as they move and forget to keep in contact.

If the team is really struggling, you may want to give them the option to regain a stepping stone by telling you a specific example of when they saw that strength being utilized during the activity.

3. DEBRIEF: SMALL GROUP QUESTIONS (15 MINUTES)

Objective: To engage student discussion on the effects of different positive behaviors on group success.

Setup: Break into groups of three.

1. Have students discuss the following questions (for 5 to 10 minutes):
    * Think of the words that you wrote on your stepping stones. What positive personal and group qualities led to your success?

- Why are these important when working in a group?
- What is the most important thing you learned in this activity? How can you apply this to other activities?

2. Have the small groups report back on the third question.

Lesson 19

Healthy Relationships
Consensus

ACTIVITIES ⚽

1. Velcro Circle (10 minutes)
2. Blind Shape (15 minutes)
3. Blind Polygon (15 minutes)
4. Debrief: One-Word Whip (5 minutes)

MATERIALS ✍

- Blindfolds (one per person)
- One long rope tied in a loop

---

1. VELCRO CIRCLE (10 MINUTES)

Objective: To warm students up to the idea of moving with their eyes closed.

Setup: Gather the students together for instructions. Make sure that your playing space is clear of obstacles.

Framing: Say to students: "In this activity, you will have the opportunity to take into account the three different comfort zones, and you will help keep each other safe."

1. Gather the group into a "Velcro circle"—a circle so tight that if students had Velcro on their shoulders, they would stick together.

2. Explain that each player is going to have an exchange with both of his/her immediate neighbors. The conversation replays the phrases from an earlier game, How Do You Do? The response is always, "Fine, thanks." This conversation should go on until everyone has asked and responded several times.

3. Explain that *muddling* is a special walk that students will have a chance to do. Muddling is how penguins walk, with their feet close together and their "hands" (wings) up in front of them.

4. Ask students to close their eyes. Remind them of their responsibility to take care of themselves—in this case, to peek—if they are entering their panic zone.

5. Instruct students to turn out from the circle, with their eyes closed, and to muddle until you yell, "Stop!" This will allow students to scatter. Monitor everyone for safety (muddling will keep them from walking too fast).

6. Call out "Stop!" and inform students that their next challenge is to re-form exactly their original circle, still keeping their eyes closed. Their only method of identifying their original neighbors in the circle is by using the phrases "How do you do?" and "Fine, thanks."
7. Students may open their eyes when the whole group believes that everyone is in the right place.

Safety Check
Be sure that the group is ready to do this eyes-closed activity. It is also important to know that they will stop when you ask them. Remind students to muddle slowly so as not to run into anyone else or any other objects.

2. BLIND SHAPE (15 MINUTES)

Objective: To make a variety of shapes using a rope while blindfolded.
Setup: Lay rope on the floor in a circle (tied at both ends with a secure knot) and ask students to circle up. Pass out blindfolds (one per person). Once they are blindfolded, ask students to pick up the rope with both hands, being careful not to tug on the rope.
Framing: Say to students: "Over this year, we've looked at the importance of trusting each other, good communication, and building our problem-solving skills. Our activities today will have you working with your eyes closed, so you won't be able to see each other or even the task you are working on."

1. The task is to create different shapes with the rope. Everyone must keep at least one hand on the rope at all times. When they think they have made the correct shape (by consensus), they can check their work by lowering their blindfolds.
2. Start with making a circle, just to get the idea. Then progress through two to four more challenging shapes (e.g., square, equilateral triangle, trapezoid). You or the students can then choose shapes.

Safety Check
Student should not pull forcefully on the rope!
Watch that students do not walk into each other or the furniture while blindfolded.

Facilitation Tips
As a lead-in to Blind Polygon, you can ask students what strategies they used to be successful.

3. BLIND POLYGON (15 MINUTES)

Objective: To create a "perfect" polygon while blindfolded.
Setup: Same as Blind Shape.
Framing: Say to students: "Your next challenge is to form a *perfect* polygon with the blindfolds on again."

1. Have students put bandanas back on and pick the ropes back up, being careful not to tug on the rope.
2. Students should agree that their polygon is perfect before they remove their blindfolds.

Safety Check
Student should not pull forcefully on the rope to avoid rope burn.
Watch that students do not walk into each other or the furniture while blindfolded.

Facilitation Tips
Students sometimes get frustrated about what a "perfect" polygon means. If they ask, "Do we have one yet?" refer them back to the group to make their decision. They can check their work by taking off their blindfolds once they have all agreed.

4. DEBRIEF: ONE-WORD WHIP (5 MINUTES)

1. Ask students to form a circle.
2. Pose each of the following questions and limit the students' responses to only one word (or phrase):
   - One word to rate the group's ability to arrive at a decision.
   - One word to explain how this might change how you make future decisions.

Lesson 20

Healthy Relationships
Empathy

<table>
<tr><td>

ACTIVITIES ⚽

1. Balloon Frantic (10 minutes)
2. Protector (25 minutes)
3. Debrief: Pair Share (10 minutes)

</td><td>

MATERIALS ✍

- Easy-to-blow balloons (one balloon per student, plus spares)
- Spot marker (one per student)
- Fleece ball (one)

</td></tr>
</table>

1. BALLOON FRANTIC (10 MINUTES)

Objective: To keep everybody's balloons juggling in the air.

Setup: Clear a large open space indoors. Ask students to blow up their own balloons. Everyone starts scattered in this open space with their own balloon in hand.

Framing: Say to students: "This is an opportunity for you to practice setting a group goal and evaluate that goal. You will be juggling everyone's balloons, so you can't just focus on your own."

1. The group should set a goal as to how many balloons they can keep up in the air simultaneously before handling any balloons.
2. On "Go," each student in the group is to hit their balloon into the air. Balloons must remain in the air at all times. Once a balloon touches the ground, the group should start a new round.
3. The group should monitor their own touches.
4. Give the group a few minutes to meet or exceed their initial goal. Then call time and ask them to develop better strategies and to restate their goal if they need to change it in any way.

Safety Check

Be sure that the ground is free from obstructions and that the playing area is large and high enough.

Ask students to be careful not to make wild gestures with their feet and hands in an attempt to keep a balloon up. No one wants to be punched or kicked!

Facilitation Tips

If the group cannot self-monitor their behavior and their "fouls," you may need to ask for volunteers to help you monitor the group.

Have extra balloons around to replace the inevitable popped ones!

2. PROTECTOR (25 MINUTES)

Objective: To experience being the protector of someone as well as the one targeted.

Setup: Have students circle up. Place a spot marker at the feet of each person. Choose one person to be the Protectee and one to be the Bodyguard.

Framing: Say to students: "This is a form of tag, but one in which there are three different roles to play. Ideally, each of you should experience each of the three roles. Consider what needs you have regarding taking risks as well as what others can do to help you."

1. Define the three roles in the game:
   - Throwers: Work together as a team to tag the Protectee by throwing the ball at them.
   - Bodyguard: Block/deflect the ball to guard the Protectee.
   - Protectee: Working with the Bodyguard, avoid contact with the fleece ball.
2. Throwers must have one foot on the spot in order to throw and cannot step into the circle at any time.
3. Throwers can pass the ball to anyone on their team at any time.
4. Throwers must throw at the Protectee below the shoulder; otherwise the "tag" does not count.
5. Protectee is considered tagged if the ball hits them anywhere below the shoulders on a fly. Bounce shots are not "legal" tags.
6. Bodyguard can block the ball, but cannot throw the ball away from the Throwers.
7. Roles will be rotated as follows: Thrower who made the "tag" becomes the Protectee, Protectee becomes the Bodyguard, and the Bodyguard becomes a Thrower.

Safety Check

Be sure to use a soft throwing object and emphasize throwing below shoulder height.

Be sure the ground is even and free of obstructions because the two middle players move around quickly.

Facilitation Tips

The middle two players can become very fatigued; consider rotating positions whenever this occurs.

Optional Questions:

- Which role did you enjoy the most? Why?
- What did the protector do for you in this activity? When do you play this role in life?
- When might you want a protector?

3. DEBRIEF: PAIR SHARE (10 MINUTES)

1. Define empathy with the whole group.
2. Have students pair up and discuss the following questions:
   - How was empathy present in the activities today?
   - Where do you experience empathy in your everyday life?
   - What makes it easy for you to give and receive empathy? What makes it difficult?
3. Gather students and ask a few to report out on their discussion.

Lesson 21

Healthy Relationships
Trust Sequence IV

ACTIVITIES ☻	MATERIALS ✎
1. Everybody's Up (15 minutes) 2. Levitation (25 minutes) 3. Debrief: Continuum (5 minutes)	• None

1. EVERYBODY'S UP (15 MINUTES)

Objective: Students to stand up from a seated position working with partners.
Setup: Ask your students to circle up.
Framing: Say to students: "There are things in life you just can't do on your own. In this activity you need other people's help to reach your goal. We are coming back to this activity to see if we can take it a step or two further."

1. Have the group get into pairs.
2. Have each pair start sitting face to face and with toes touching. Students clasp hands or arms and get up in this position.
3. When they are ready, students can attempt to stand up as a pair.
4. Once they have succeeded, have two pairs join so that the groups are four people, and have them attempt to stand up together.
5. Have each group of four add another pair.
6. Keep adding to the groups to see how large a group can stand using only one another to push against for support.

Safety Check
Make sure people are aware of any preexisting wrist, arm, or shoulder injuries before attempting.

Facilitation Tips
Students should enjoy themselves, but keep in mind this is a serious activity and should be treated as such.

2. LEVITATION (25 MINUTES)

Objective: To build trust and have students support each other.

Framing: Say to students: "Does everyone know what levitation is? Well, today we will all get a chance to experience it if we choose."

1. Ask for a volunteer to lie on the ground, face up.
2. The rest of the group should place their hands under the volunteer's body. One person should be assigned to the person's head.
3. Pick a leader (who should be you in the first round). The leader calls out the commands for each round of the activity. The leader asks if the volunteer is ready. If the volunteer answers yes, then the leader asks, "Lifters ready?" The group responds accordingly.
4. When everyone is ready, on the leader's count, the group lifts the volunteer to waist level. It is important that the volunteer remain very stiff and still.
5. Depending on the group and the volunteer's comfort level, she can be raised higher, even going as high as shoulder level.
6. On the leader's count, the volunteer is then slowly lowered, with a gentle rocking motion added to the descent, until she is safely on the ground.

Safety Check
Challenge by Choice is essential in this activity.

Make sure the volunteer's head stays even with the rest of the body and that the body stays level. Remind people that a person's torso is heavier than the legs. Position more people to lift in the torso area.

Facilitation Tips
Allow the group to lift the volunteer higher only if given permission to do so.

You may have the group turn in a 360-degree circle after the person is raised.

Doing this in silence makes for a very peaceful experience.

3. DEBRIEF: CONTINUUM (5 MINUTES)

Objective: To help students quickly reflect on the trust they have built over the year to date.

Framing: Say to students: "We are going to use an imaginary continuum to think about trust in our group."

1. Designate a continuum of success across the room. One end will be A and the other B (see the figure below).

2. With each question, have students place themselves along the continuum, and check in with individual students as required.
    - What was scarier for you, (A) lifting people or (B) being lifted?
    - Was this activity more about (A) physical or (B) emotional risks?
    - Did the group influence you (A) positively or (B) negatively?
    - Rate yourself (A = High, B = Low) in terms of trusting the group at the start of the year. Rate yourself how you now trust the group.
    - Rate yourself (A = High, B = Low) in terms of how trustworthy you think you were at the start of the year. Then rate yourself now.

Facilitation Tips

Depending on time, you may engage in a discussion of how trust is built, where it is important in students' lives, how physical and emotional risks differ, and how students are (and can be) trustworthy.

Lesson 22

Healthy Relationships
Negotiation

ACTIVITIES ⚽	MATERIALS ✎
1. Psychic Handshake (5 minutes)	• None
2. Orient the Square (5 minutes)	
3. Negotiation Square (25 minutes)	
4. Debrief: Human Camera (10 minutes)	

---

1. PSYCHIC HANDSHAKE (5 MINUTES)

Objective: A fun way to split up the group.
Setup: Ask the students to circle up.

1. Explain that you are going to ask students to pick a number (only one) in their head between one and four. They cannot change their number.
2. Students cannot communicate, verbally or otherwise, to anyone else what their number is before the activity begins.
3. Students will mingle and try to find their group by shaking hands with other students. Each student will shake their own hand corresponding to the number they are thinking of, and so will their partner.
4. Explain that the key to this activity is for each student to hold their arm firm when they accomplish the required number of shakes. "So, if you are thinking 'three' and I'm thinking 'two,' we will happily shake each other's hands for the first two shakes, and then suddenly my arm will go stiff and prevent any further shakes."
5. Once each student has a number in mind, invite them to mingle and shake hands in a friendly manner. When they encounter other people with the same number, they can stick together as a group.
6. At the end of the activity, you may end up with different-sized groups. Ask for volunteers in larger groups to join smaller groups to have four groups of approximately the same size.

Safety Check
Emphasize "friendly" handshakes. This activity is about trying to guess the handshake number, not squishing your partner's hand.

Facilitation Tips
It's a good idea to demonstrate what the "shaking of hands" and "holding firm" positions look like—in front of everyone before you say "Go"—to give everyone a clue.

2. ORIENT THE SQUARE (5 MINUTES)

Objective: To follow instructions and maintain the correct square position in relation to the leader.
Setup: Have the students form a square, each side being comprised by one of the small groups from the previous activity. Place yourself in the center of the square, clearly facing one of the "sides."
Framing: Say to students: "Your challenge in this activity is to work as a team and maintain the square in relative orientation to me. As I change directions, you must reorient according to where you were in relation to me."

1. Explain that you will turn directions and the square needs to reorganize itself exactly as it is as quickly as possible. That is, students facing your front should still be in front of you and those on your left should still be on your left.
2. Start with small rotations (e.g., 45 degrees) and build toward bigger turns.

Safety Check
Make sure the space you are working in is clear of objects, and remind students to be mindful of each other as they change places.

Facilitation Tips
This activity is primarily done for fun and sets up the group for the following activity.

3. NEGOTIATION SQUARE (25 MINUTES)

Objective: To negotiate with other small groups and arrive at a common group symbol and sound.
Setup: Have groups stay in the square from the previous activity.
Framing: Say to students: "This activity will test your powers of negotiation and psychic energy!"

1. Ask each group to step away from the square and, privately, to create a motion accompanied by a sound that will represent their group. This motion and sound need to be easily learned and repeated by others.
2. Ask the groups to come back to the square. One at a time, each group will demonstrate their motion and sound. Ask the other groups to learn and practice each motion and sound that is presented.

3. Ask each group to once again step away from the square. The groups must now decide on one of the four motions and sounds they have learned that they will do next. The goal of this activity is for the entire class to do the same motion and sound simultaneously, without planning or communicating with the other groups.

4. When each group has decided quietly what they are going to do, have the square come back together. On the count of three, everyone does the motion they chose.

5. In rare instances, the whole class will do the same motion the first time. If not, have the groups continue the activity until the class all performs the same motion.

6. Observe how the class does or does not negotiate. Remember, groups may not talk to each other!

Safety Check

No specific safety procedures required for this activity.

Facilitation Tips

If the groups arrive at the same motion and sound in the first round or so, do the activity again with new groups, new motions, and new sounds!

If it takes groups a while to coordinate, observe their frustration and intervene only if necessary. They do eventually get it, so be patient.

Debrief Questions

In small groups, discuss:

• Did the class manage to negotiate easily? Why or why not?
• What can we learn from this about negotiating with other groups in school, or with others in this group?

Then share what was learned as a large group as time allows. If needed you could ask for one or two examples.

4. DEBRIEF: HUMAN CAMERA (10 MINUTES)

Objective: To reflect on the concept of negotiation while working in pairs.

Setup: Ask students to form pairs.

Framing: Say to students: "Each of you will have the opportunity to be a photographer as a camera. As the photographer, you will be looking around the classroom to capture a snapshot that in some way represents *negotiation*."

1. The photographer's task is to capture a photograph that represents *negotiation*. Their partner will act as the Human Camera.

2. Give everyone about one minute to walk around the classroom to visualize their snapshot.

3. Once the group has returned, have pairs designate who will be the first photographer and who will be the first camera.
4. The first photographer will lead the Human Camera with their eyes closed to his or her snapshot.
5. Once the photographer is in front of the snapshot, they should carefully position the camera's head so that, when they open their eyes, they will be looking directly at the designated photograph.
6. A picture is taken by gently tapping the head of the camera. When this happens, the camera quickly opens and closes their eyes to get a snapshot view of what is in front of them.
7. The partners then change roles and repeat the above steps.

Safety Check

Assess that the students are ready to lead each other around independently.

Ask students to commit to taking care of their unsighted partners.

Designate a specific area that students should avoid and limit the traveling area if necessary.

Goal Setting

Evaluating Goals and Setting Long-Term Goals

ACTIVITIES ⚽	MATERIALS ✍
1. Goal Pair Share (10 minutes) 2. Mass Pass (30 minutes) 3. Debrief: Bucket Voting (5 minutes)	• Mass Pass kit • Rubber chicken

1. GOAL PAIR SHARE (10 MINUTES)

Objective: To review student goals set after winter break.

Setup: Hand out student goal sheets created during Lesson 17 and ask students to pair up.

Framing: Say to students: "Goals are only useful if you come back to them to help motivate you to stretch yourself and to check in on your progress. In this activity we will review the goals you have set."

Have students review their goals and discuss their progress with their partners, considering the following questions:

• What steps have they taken in getting closer to their goal?
• Are they still motivated by a desire to achieve this goal? If not, ask them to rephrase their goal.
• What next steps do they need to take to work toward their current goal?

2. MASS PASS (30 MINUTES)

Objective: To successfully pass as many objects as possible to reach a self-determined goal.

Setup: Using rope, create a fairly large square (15 to 25 feet per side). Make sure that the square has clearly defined corners. In one corner of the square, place one bucket (bucket #1), and in the opposite corner place the other bucket (bucket #2). Place all the fleece balls, foam balls, and rubber chicken into bucket #1.

Framing: Say to students: "This activity requires you to transport multiple objects around the perimeter of the square. The ability to plan effectively is needed to succeed, yet there is also opportunity for creative thinking in devising a strategy. I'll give you all the rules, and then I'll give you some time to plan."

1. The goal for the group is to increase their score over several (maximum of six) successive rounds and to maximize their score in the last round. Give the following rules and then allow for some planning time. Points are scored according to how many objects end up in bucket #2 over a 90-second period (round).
2. All objects must start inside bucket #1 at the beginning of every round.
3. Time for each round starts when the first object is removed from bucket #1.
4. All sides of the square must be occupied by at least one student.
5. Once a person has chosen a side of the square to stand on, she or he may not switch sides within a round.
6. Every participant must touch each object after it leaves bucket #1 and before it ends up in bucket #2.
7. Objects may not be passed to anyone to the immediate right or left; in other words, the object must "skip" at least one person when it is passed.
8. Points are earned for each object that is placed successfully in bucket #2.
9. Whenever an object is being passed, it must always cross over the inside of the boundary area (i.e., it cannot be passed around the corner outside the perimeter of the square or behind anyone).
10. Whenever an object is dropped outside the boundary marker, it must be returned to the "resource container" (bucket #1) to be recycled if it is to be used in the round.
11. If an object is dropped inside the boundary markers, it may not be retrieved and is lost for the duration of that round.
12. No member of the team may step inside the perimeter boundary during a round. If this occurs, all objects must be returned to the starting bucket.
13. All actions must stop when the time is up. At that time, students should count the objects in bucket #2 and tally their score.
14. Scoring: 10 points for every fleece ball, 20 points for every foam ball.
15. Give timed (one-minute) planning opportunities between each round so that the class can continually improve their time.
16. Conduct three or more rounds.

Facilitation Tips

To increase the challenge level of this activity, include different objects with different point values—for example, include a rubber chicken that is worth 50 points.

Look for the following themes emerging: idea generation, time management, creative problem solving, listening, and inclusion. Use these to generate questions for the debrief.

3. DEBRIEF: BUCKET VOTING (5 MINUTES)

Setup: Give each student a ball and place buckets in two distinct areas.

1. Consider the themes that emerged in Mass Pass.
2. Tell the students that each bucket will represent a vote or answer to a question you will ask.
3. Once you have posed the question, ask students to vote by throwing their ball into a bucket.
4. Identifying the bucket with the most votes is then fairly simple.

Facilitation Tips

Questions may include:

- How successful were you in achieving your goals (not very or very successful)?
- Did you feel included in the planning process (yes or no)?
- How good of a listener/supporter were you in this activity (good or not good)?

It is important to create a safe space for those members whose vote falls outside the majority of the group. Rather than saying, "Hey, who voted 'not very' when the rest of us voted 'very successful'?" ask the group, "Can you imagine how someone could vote the other way for this last activity?"

Lesson 24

Leadership
What Is Leadership?

ACTIVITIES ☻	MATERIALS ✍
1. Car and Driver (10 minutes)	• Cones
2. Don't Break the Ice (25 minutes)	• Blindfolds for half the group (optional)
3. Debrief: Leadership Pi Chart (10 minutes)	• Flip chart paper or whiteboard
	• Assorted markers
	• Long rope
	• Stepping stones (one per student)

1. CAR AND DRIVER (10 MINUTES)

Objective: To understand what it means to be responsible for someone else and conversely to appreciate what goes into being a follower.

Setup: Find a large playing area, a gym or a field. Set up a series of cones that represent a road for the cars and drivers to go on. Partner up the students.

Framing: Say to students: "In this activity you will have the chance to be a driver of a very expensive car. Your job is to keep this car from bumping into anything, steering it clear of all obstacles, including other cars."

1. Before introducing the rules of this game, ask the students what they think the safety considerations should be in playing a game with their eyes closed.
2. The pace will be slow. Students always are allowed to "peek" if they need to.
3. Set up the pairs so that one student is standing in front of the other. The student in front is the car, and the student in the back is the driver. The student who is the "car" should have their hands up as bumpers.
4. Drivers will guide their cars by placing their hands on the shoulders of the cars, as well as by using verbal communication.
5. Have the students enter the preset "roadway" so that there is at least 15 feet of space between partners.

6. Drivers are to safely "drive" their cars through the course.
7. Once the students have completed the course, they may wish to switch roles if time allows.

Safety Check

Offer blindfolds, but give students the choice of shutting their eyes.
Play in an area that is free from obstacles.

Facilitation Tips

Give students a choice of using only verbal instructions. This is helpful to those who are uncomfortable with physical touch.

Optional Questions:

- What did it feel like to be a driver? To be a car?
- Which did you like best and why?

2. DON'T BREAK THE ICE (25 MINUTES)

Objective: To get the whole group to stand on the "ice" as pieces melt away.
Setup: Create a circle or other unique shape with the rope, making sure that it is enclosed. Spread out the stepping stones inside your new shape, making sure that no two stepping stones are touching.
Framing: Say to students: "Your group is crossing a frozen lake. However, due to global warming, the lake is melting and you can only step on the ice 'spots.' You must get your entire group onto the ice spots without touching the water, because if you do, you could freeze and everyone has to return to shore to administer first aid. If this happens, the group will then have to start over."

1. Ensure that all students understand they must get on the ice spots and return to shore without touching the "water" to be successful.
2. Any time a group member touches the water, the entire group starts over.
3. The ice spots cannot be slid across the ground.
4. At the end of each successful round, the group can increase the challenge by deciding to remove one ice spot from the lake and move another spot to a new location to make the task achievable. Students should use Decision Thumbs in making these choices.
5. The next round is conducted in the same way; all students must get on and off the ice spots without touching the water.
6. The activity continues until the group can no longer perform the task dues to lack of ice spots.

Safety Check

No piggybacks or handstands.

Facilitation Tips

To help students stick with Decision Thumbs, only the teacher can move or remove "ice" from the lake. Ensure that the request being made by students was actually achieved by consensus.

3. DEBRIEF: LEADERSHIP PI CHART (10 MINUTES)

Objective: To gain a deeper understanding of the concept of leadership.

Framing: Say to students: "One thing that we've identified over the year as helping our group be successful is leadership. Sometimes, leadership is clearly defined as in the activity Car and Driver. Sometimes leadership is not clearly defined and arises from within the group. Let's think more about what leadership means to us."

1. Explain to your students that the same word may have different meanings for different people.
2. Draw the following figure on whiteboard, poster board, or flip chart paper:

LEADERSHIP		
LOOKS LIKE	FEELS LIKE	SOUNDS LIKE

3. The group should then brainstorm what leadership looks like, feels like, and sounds like. There are no right or wrong answers; this is just how people think of the word. Write down anything that comes up. Try not to talk over each other. It is OK if you need to add more structure to this brainstorm though, perhaps using a talking stick or raising hands.

Using the word leadership as an example:
- It might *look like* everyone looking at and listening to one person.
- It might *feel like* people value your ideas and that you are an important part of the solution.
- It might *sound like* someone suggesting an idea or organizing the group to try out an idea.

4. Once you've begun to fill in the chart, lead a discussion about what's been written thus far. This is time for students to explain what they meant, to ask for clarity, and to come to some degree of consensus. You won't want to spend a great deal of time on this, just enough to have the group understand and agree on some common language, actions, and feelings, but not so much time that your students become bored and disengaged. You will recognize that it's time to move on when the conversational momentum dwindles.

Lesson 25

Leadership

Leadership and Followership

ACTIVITIES ⚽

1. Front/Back/Left/Right (5 minutes)
2. Instigator (10 minutes)
3. Pitfall (25 minutes)
4. Debrief: Pitfall Objects (5 minutes)

MATERIALS ✍

- Long rope
- Variety of random objects (rubber chickens, foam balls, fleece balls, spots, etc.) (30+)

---

1. FRONT/BACK/LEFT/RIGHT (5 MINUTES)

Objective: To warm students up and introduce an element of confusion and fun.
Setup: Ask students to stand in a wide circle.
Framing: Say to students: "Today's activities are going to require some quick thinking. To get our brains warmed up we're going to start with a short activity."

1. Explain that students need to repeat a direction you give (Front, Back, Left, Right) and make a small hop in that direction.
2. Do a few rounds of Front, Back, Left, Right, Front, Front, Left, etc., until the students figure it out.
3. Round 2: Students say the opposite and do the opposite motion (e.g., Teacher says "Back," students say "Front" and hop forward).
4. Round 3: Students say the opposite and do the correct motion (e.g., Teacher says "Back," students say "Front" and hop backward).

Safety Check
Choose appropriate jumping directions when in constricted spaces.

2. INSTIGATOR (10 MINUTES)

Objective: To explore the concept of followership.
Setup: Any comfortable space will do. Students should be standing, ready to "mill" about.

Framing: Say to students: "This activity will test your skills of observation, of picking up on subtleties, and will help you understand some of the characteristics of being a follower."

1. One person will be asked to leave the room or the area where the rest of the group is located. This person is designated the "detector."
2. The class then selects one person to be the "instigator."
3. The activity is quite simple; everyone mills about mimicking the instigator. Whatever the instigator does, everyone does.
4. However, the instigator is charged with making his/her changes in movement very subtle because the detector will try to determine who the instigator is when they return.
5. The activity begins when the detector rejoins the group. She/he observes the group until they can identify who the instigator is.
6. Reminder: the rest of the class should be subtle in their imitation in order to make it difficult for the detector to ID the instigator. Not everyone should be staring at the instigator.

Facilitation Tips
Optional Questions:

- Was it easy to follow the instigator? Is following generally easy to do?
- Does it differ for different people and in different circumstances?

3. PITFALL (25 MINUTES)

Objective: To verbally guide a blindfolded partner through the "pitfall" course.
Setup: Using the long rope, mark a large rectangle (about 15 by 25 feet) on the ground. Scatter objects (balls, stuffed animals, spots, etc.) inside the boundary so that it is not easy to walk from one end to the other without stepping on an object (see the figure below). Ask students to get into pairs.

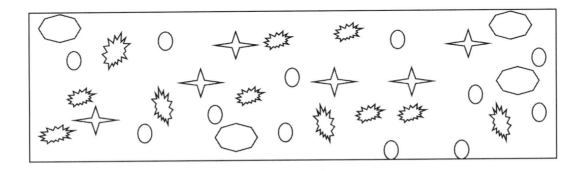

Framing: Say to students: "This is a blindfold activity. One partner will be 'leading' the unsighted partner through the pit. Think about our Full Value Contract and how it will help you take the risk of entering the pit unsighted."

1. Show the class the variety of objects that are in the pit.
2. Have each pair decide who in the partnership will be blindfolded and who will be the guide.
3. The object is for all the unsighted students to successfully get from one end of the rectangle to the other without touching any objects.
4. The guide may not touch their partner or enter the pit.
5. The class is to add up the number of touches that each person made, attempting to get as few touches as possible as a whole class.
6. After the first partner is done, the pair is to have a brief discussion as to what was or was not effective about the guide's strategy.
7. Partners change roles and repeat the above.
8. Blindfolded students are to enter the rectangle at one end and exit at the other.
9. Start pairs off with a 30-second delay between pairs to avoid a traffic jam.

Safety Check

Have the person walking through the pit keep their bumpers up (arms slightly bent, hands up to protect themselves).

Remind students that they are responsible for the safety of their blindfolded partners.

Facilitation Tips

Students can choose whether they want to use a blindfold or simply close their eyes.

Optional: You can also allow guides to enter the pit with their partners.

4. DEBRIEF: PITFALL OBJECTS (5 MINUTES)

Setup: Using the obstacle objects from Pitfall. Have students stand around the perimeter of the pit.

1. Ask students to reflect on both followership and leadership and to pick an object in their mind that represents each and something significant they learned in this activity. Students should then share what two objects they picked and why with their partner.
2. They should not pick up objects so all students can look at the range of objects when drawing their connections.

Lesson 26

Problem Solving
Review ABCDE Model

ACTIVITIES ⚽	MATERIALS ✍
1. Your Add (5 minutes) 2. Keypunch (30 minutes) 3. Debrief: Plus/Delta (10 minutes)	• Keypunch set (30 numbered spots) • Ropes for circular boundary • Start/finish lines • ABCDE handout (copy from Appendix F) • Keypunch Rules handout (copy from Appendix J) • Plus/Delta handout—one per student (copy from Appendix K)

1. YOUR ADD (5 MINUTES)

Objective: To quickly add up the sum of fingers showing (thrown) between two dueling players.
Setup: Have students pair up.
Framing: Say to students: "Sometimes we have to react quickly in problem solving. This game will test your reaction time."

1. Have pairs face each other.
2. To initiate the start of the game, one of the pair calls out, "Set." At this point, each person places their hands behind their backs and extends a number of fingers (that only they will know). Options vary between 0 (both hands are clenched) to 10 (all fingers and thumbs are extended).
3. When the second person is ready, they will call out, "Go." Together, each partner brings their hands in front with the number of fingers extended.
4. With all four hands visible, the first person to say the total number of all fingers extended (for both players) is the winner. For example, if you extend six fingers and your partner shows three, the first person to call "nine" wins.

Facilitation Tips

This game works best if people simply mingle about in a space, and once someone spies a willing partner, they face off with them. This pair can engage in one or two rounds and then move on to find a new rival.

2. KEYPUNCH (30 MINUTES)

Objective: To score the fastest team time possible by making contact with the spots in sequential order.

Setup: Make a circle boundary with rope. Inside the circle place the 30 numbered spots in random order. Place some of the spots deep inside the boundary so that they cannot be reached from outside the boundary (see the figure below). (Number placement in figure is just an example. The numbers may be different every time one sets up the activity.) Place a starting line about 15 to 20 feet away. Ask the class to stand behind the line.

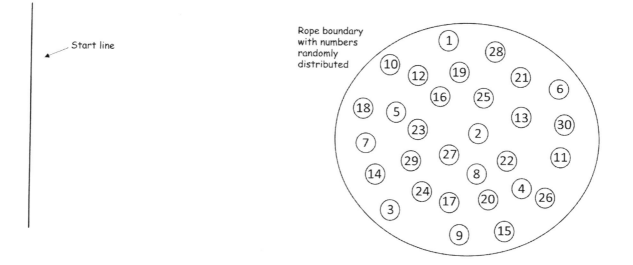

Framing: Say to students: "You have been asked here because you are experts in debugging large computer programs. The computer you are challenged to fix is set here on the ground. The best way to fix this computer and remove the bugs is to touch each number in sequence, from lowest to highest. The faster the numbers are touched, the greater the number of bugs that are removed from the program. You will be timed to see if you can remove all the bugs." Briefly remind students of the ABCDE Decision-Making process (Appendix F).

1. Hand out Keypunch Rules sheet (Appendix J) to students and give them a few minutes to read the rules.
2. Explain to students that the challenge of this activity is to work together as a group/team to score the fastest time possible by making contact with the designated spots in sequential order. Planning time is given before each round.

3. After the first round, set a goal to challenge students, i.e., to cut their time by a quarter, a third, or a half.

4. There will be three rounds, so make sure students plan between every round.

Safety Check
Be careful when stepping on the numbers, as spots might be slippery and may slide.

Facilitation Tips
Students inevitably have questions. Try to redirect their questions to the rules sheet they have. Alternatively, you can allow students to ask three questions, emphasizing that they all need to agree on the question to be asked.

Watch for more than one person within the boundary at one time and spots being stepped on out of sequence.

Add up the number of penalties and add five seconds for each.

3. DEBRIEF: PLUS/DELTA (10 MINUTES)

Objective: To review the group's success and challenges during Keypunch.

Setup: Divide the group into pairs. Hand out one copy per student of the Plus/Delta Worksheet (Appendix K).

1. Ask students to individually find two examples of pluses and two of deltas.
2. Share in pairs.
3. If time allows, have each pair share their best examples from each column with the entire group.

Lesson 27

Problem Solving
Defining Teamwork

ACTIVITIES ☻

1. Circle the Circle (10 minutes)
2. Portable Porthole (25 minutes)
3. Debrief: Passenger, Crew, Captain (10 minutes)

MATERIALS ✍

• Hula hoops (two)

---

1. CIRCLE THE CIRCLE (10 MINUTES)

Objective: To work as efficiently as possible in this physical coordination group challenge in a race against the clock.

Setup: This activity can be done either indoors or outdoors.

Ask the group to form a circle. Explain the guidelines. Hand the hula hoop to one participant. Then ask the group to join hands to close the circle, with hula hoop between the person you handed it to and their neighbor.

Framing: Say to students: "In this team challenge, we are racing the clock. Watch one another's technique so we can find the most effective and efficient way to pass the hoop around the circle."

1. The challenge is to have the hula hoop pass around the circle without anyone letting go of their team member's hands.
2. When the hula hoop has been passed around the circle once, you can now time how quickly the group is able to pass the hula hoop around the circle in the second round.
3. For Round 3, try to beat the time for Round 2 following the same instructions.
4. Variation: Introduce a second hula hoop. One hoop must travel around the circle clockwise, and the other must travel around the team circle counterclockwise.

Safety Check

Be aware of wrist or shoulder injuries when firmly clasping hands and moving quickly. Also, sometimes people could be tripped up when stepping through the hoop. Remove hazards that someone could fall into such as a desk or chair.

Facilitation Tips

Round 1 is a baseline, but you can choose to time any of the rounds and simply ask folks to show improvement in between rounds.

2. PORTABLE PORTHOLE (25 MINUTES)

Objective: To have the entire group pass through the hula hoop.
Setup: Clear an open space.
Framing: Say to students: "Your task is to get your group from one side of the porthole to the other side."

1. Two students hold up the hula hoop at a height of two to four feet. No other students may touch the hoop until one of the Holders' turn to go through. At that time, they can ask for a sub. Holders can move the hoop up or down for correct height of person passing through.
2. Once students have passed through the hula hoop, they may not return to help lift, but they can always come back to spot.

Safety Check

Remind students of correct spotting techniques and that there should always be spotters on both sides of the porthole.
Diving or jumping is not permitted.
If participants are being levitated through, proper lifting and lowering techniques must be used.

Facilitation Tips

Each participant should be invited to choose how he or she wants to go through, e.g., feet first, lifted, given a knee to step onto, etc.

3. DEBRIEF: PASSENGER, CREW, CAPTAIN (10 MINUTES)

1. Ask students to reflect on the previous activities and consider if they felt they were more of a passenger, a crew member, or a captain.
2. Have students report out popcorn style, describing which role they think best describes their role and why.

Lesson 28

Problem Solving

How I (and Others) Contribute to Our Team

ACTIVITIES ⚽	MATERIALS ✍
1. Triangle Tag (5 minutes) 2. Alphabet Soup—Fastback (30 minutes) 3. Debrief: Tic-Tac-Toe (10 minutes)	• Alphabet Soup kit (Project Adventure) • Boundary rope • Whiteboard or flip chart paper with Tic-Tac-Toe board written out

1. TRIANGLE TAG (5 MINUTES)

Objective: To warm up using a vigorous group tag game.

Setup: Select an open space. Ask students to get into groups of four.

Framing: Say to students: "This is a quick warm-up game that highlights how you can support other students."

1. Three of the four people should hold hands in a triangle. The fourth person will become "It."
2. Identify which one of the three people in the triangle is designated to be tagged and which two are the protectors of that person.
3. When the game begins, the It person can run around the other two players in the triangle to tag the designated person. The triangle group can dance and swing around to protect the designee.
4. The It person cannot intentionally break apart the grips of the other students or move through/over/under the triangle.
5. After each successful tag, or every 60 seconds or so, rotate roles. This game is a cardio workout!

Safety Check

Monitor that the person who is It doesn't become too aggressive. This is a fast-paced game, and an open area is required.

Facilitation Tips

A gym space or field is preferred, free of hazards.

2. ALPHABET SOUP—FASTBACK (30 MINUTES)

Objective: To reflect on one's own contribution to the success of the team.
Setup: Create three zones as shown in the following figure:

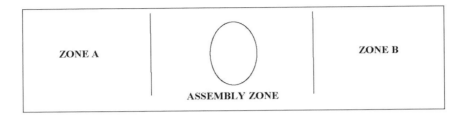

- The distance from Zones A and B to the Assembly Zone can range from 5 to 10 feet.
- Place all the foam blocks (with the cutouts removed) in Zone A.
- Place all the cutouts of the letters and numbers in Zone B.

Framing: Say to students: "Sometime life gets complicated and I need to pause and reflect on how I contribute to my team. Sometimes I even may need to take on a different role in order to support my group. Let's use this puzzle to look at our roles and our contributions."

1. The task has many variations, all requiring that the cutouts be put back into the "right" block; then the blocks get assembled in a particular order. One basic configuration is as follows (for others, see the Facilitation Tips section):
   Arrange the blocks in alphabetical order followed by numbers in numerical order. Form three rows: A–M (13 blocks), N–Z (13 blocks), and numbers zero to nine (10 blocks).
2. Separate your students into two relatively equal roles:
   - The Assemblers who must stay in the Assembly Zone at all times to put letter and number cutouts into blocks in the pattern you've specified.
   - The Resourcers who can move back and forth from Zone A and B to the Assembly Zone, but may not enter the Assembly Zone at any time.
3. When the time starts, Resourcers may bring letters, numbers, and cutouts to the Assembly Zone. Resourcers may only carry one piece at a time to prevent work-related injuries and not overwhelm the Assemblers. If a Resourcer carries more than one object, he or she must return the objects to the start zone and take a 30-second recovery break.
4. Resourcers may place the objects they carry inside the Assembly Zone. They may not help assemble the letters or step into the Assembly Zone. If either of these infractions occurs, the entire operation must stop for 10 seconds.
5. Assemblers may not reach outside of the Assembly Zone at any time. Whenever an arm or a leg or any body part crosses the boundary, a 10-second work stoppage will occur.
6. When assembling the blocks into the final shape—if blocks that should remain separated touch each other—four blocks will be removed from the assembly area, and the pieces must

be returned to either Zone A or B (depending on whether they are a cutout or a block) before they can be reused.

7. Give your group five minutes or so to plan and clarify the rules.
8. Start the action and time it.
9. Upon completion, let the students know how well they did on time.

Facilitation Tips

The challenge level of this activity can shift dramatically depending on the configuration of the final assembly. Know your group and choose a challenge that matches the class's skills and abilities. Other variations for arranging the blocks include the following:

- blocks arranged by alternating letters and numbers, right-side up and upside down
- blocks not arranged in a connected pattern, all letters and numbers assembled
- blocks arrange in reverse alphabetical and numerical order

Optional Questions:

- Keep the teams in the Assemblers and Resources groups.
- Ask them to discuss and report out to the group their answers to the following questions:
  ○ What did you enjoy about being a _____ (Assembler/Resourcer)?
  ○ What did you find frustrating about being a _____ (Assembler/Resourcer)?
  ○ What do you think your group did well?
  ○ What do you think you could improve on?
  ○ Overall, how do you think the larger team did?
  ○ Did people have specific roles within their groups? If so, what were they?
  ○ What roles and responsibilities do we have on our team or in our classroom that help us be successful and reach our goals?
- Give students 5 to 10 minutes and report out to the group.

3. DEBRIEF: TIC-TAC-TOE (10 MINUTES)

Setup: Draw the Tic-Tac-Toe in the figure below on a whiteboard or on flip chart paper.

Asked for Help	Really Listened to Someone Else	Tried a New Way
Shared My Ideas	Brain-Stormed	Tried it Again
Stretched Beyond My Comfort Zone	Learned Something New	Supported Someone Else

Framing: Say to students: "In pairs, please discuss the following events by choosing any that create a line of three in a row. For example, if you pick the middle row going top to bottom, share examples from today where you may have listened to someone (tell about it), brainstormed (what was your contribution?), and learned something new (what was it?)."

1. Have students reflect in pairs on the three areas in the Tic-Tac-Toe.
2. Let students know when you are halfway through the time (approximately two minutes) to allow time for each student to share.

Lesson 29

Communication
Effective Communication

ACTIVITIES ☺

1. Back-to-Back Draw (5 minutes)
2. Bridge It (35 minutes)
3. Debrief: Headliners (5 minutes)

MATERIALS ✍

- Copies of Back-to-Back Draw illustrations—one per pair (copy from Appendix L)
- Blank paper (one per student)
- Assorted pens and markers
- Construction materials for bridge. Example supplies could be: 6 cups, 10 straws, masking tape, 12 small Legos, 6 large Legos, cardboard or thick cardstock in 8.5 × 11 sheets (four), plus one toy car to test bridge at end of exercise.

---

1. BACK-TO-BACK DRAW (5 MINUTES)

Objective: This exercise helps to teach students the importance of clear and direct communication.

Setup: Have a Back-to-Back Draw handout for each pair (Appendix L) and a writing utensil/blank paper. Please note the illustrations are two pages for the two rounds.

Framing: Say to students: "This activity helps to highlight the importance of clear communication. In pairs, you are going to try to reproduce a drawing your partner will describe to you."

Round 1

1. Split the group into pairs and have partners sit back to back.
2. In the first round, give one person in the pair the picture, and give the other person a blank piece of paper and writing utensil.
3. Have the person with the picture give directions to the other person on how to redraw the picture.

4. The person drawing the picture may not ask questions.
5. Once they think the drawing is complete, have them compare it with the initial one.

Round 2

6. Have the pairs switch tasks; the person with the picture in the first round now has the blank paper and writing utensil, and the person with the blank paper has a new picture. Use the second handout. Again, have the pairs sit back to back.
7. Have the person with the picture give directions to his or her partner on drawing the picture, but this time, the person drawing the picture may ask questions.

Facilitation Tips
Print illustrations on single-sided copies so the Round 2 drawer does not get a sneak peek.

2. BRIDGE IT (35 MINUTES)

Objective: Using only the materials provided, each team must construct one half of a bridge.

Setup: Divide the class into two teams. Designate two working areas that are separate from each other in which teams will do their construction. A third neutral area is also necessary for the negotiation sessions. Materials should be distributed evenly, and each group should have the exact same resources.

Framing: Say to students: "Using only the materials provided, each team must construct one half of a bridge. When the two portions of bridge are brought together they must meet and look as identical as possible. Part of the challenge in this activity is that your two teams must do most of their design work and all of their construction in isolation from one another and with only limited communication."

1. All the materials must be used and clearly visible in the final product.
2. When completed and brought together, the two portions of the bridge must meet in the middle and look identical.
3. The time frame for the activity is as follows:
   • five minutes—examine material and brainstorming of possible designs
   • three minutes—negotiation session #1
   • five minutes—construction period
   • three minutes—negotiation session #2
   • five minutes—construction period
   • three minutes—negotiation session #3
   • five minutes—final construction period
   • Unveiling—bring the bridge halves together

Facilitation Tips
Negotiation Sessions:

- Communication between the two teams can take place only during the negotiation sessions. One person from each team represents their team at the negotiation session. A new team representative should be chosen for each negotiation session.
- Representatives from each group will meet three times in the course of the activity. Their job is to communicate the current status of the bridge construction and to negotiate any necessary modifications to ensure that the final product created by each subgroup meets the building specifications.
- Building materials may not be brought to or made during the negotiation sessions.
- Written notes may not be brought to the negotiations, nor may written notes be made.

3. DEBRIEF: HEADLINERS (5 MINUTES)

1. Ask students to imagine they needed to write an article for tonight's homework for the school or local newspaper. The article would be about today's lesson and how they worked together as a group.
2. Before they leave the circle we want to know what the headline would be for each of their articles.
3. If a student wants to pass, come back to them at the end.

Lesson 30

Problem Solving

Performing as a Team

ACTIVITIES ⚽	MATERIALS ✍
1. Tarp Toss (10 minutes) 2. Turn over a New Leaf (25 minutes) 3. Debrief: Concentric Circles (10 minutes)	• Small tarps (two) • Rubber chickens/pigs and other tossable items (have multiple items for each small group)

1. TARP TOSS (10 MINUTES)

Objective: To work in small teams and use a tarp to launch an object and use the other tarp to catch it.

Setup: Choose a space outdoors or a room with a very high ceiling (such as a gym). Split the students into two groups and give each a small tarp.

Framing: Say to students: "We are going to test how coordinated each group is! I will be giving you a series of instructions that each group must execute."

1. Start each group with their own rubber pig/chicken or stuffed animal. Have groups practice throwing and catching their own item using the tarp. Everyone must keep one hand on the tarp at all times. All catches and throws are done using the tarps.
2. Have each group demonstrate their highest toss.
3. Have each group demonstrate the highest number of consecutive tosses they can make.
4. Each group is challenged to toss their object to another group, as well as to receive an object from that other group. You can keep score of how many successful throws and catches each group makes if that seems appropriate.

Safety Check

Use objects that are relatively light and soft so if they hit someone it does not result in injury.

2. TURN OVER A NEW LEAF (25 MINUTES)

Objective: To turn over the tarp while standing on it without having any of the group members step off.

Setup: Set out tarp on a flat surface without obstructions around the tarp in case someone were to lose their balance.

Framing: Say to students: "In this challenge we have to think outside of the box while working as a team. We need everyone's help to make this work."

1. Ask each student to reflect on a personal goal they would like to work on for the rest of the year, and have them write this on a strip of masking tape.
2. Students can tape their goal on the tarp and read other students' goals.
3. Ask students for observations about what they have read.
4. Flip the tarp over so that all the goals are against the floor and the blank surface is up.
5. Ask all the students to stand on the tarp.
6. Say to students: "You may not step off of the tarp or touch the ground around the tarp at any point in time during the activity."
7. The activity is complete when the tarp is completely flipped over with the goals facing up without having stepped off at any point during the flip.
8. Have students set a natural consequence if someone steps off the tarp and hold them accountable to it.

Safety Check

Be mindful that the tarp can be slippery—especially depending on the surface underneath the tarp (e.g., waxed floors).

3. DEBRIEF: CONCENTRIC CIRCLES (10 MINUTES)

Setup: Starting with the group in one big circle, identify one person and then invite every other person to step to the center of the circle to create an inner ring. Ask the inner ring to turn so that they face the outer ring, and to align themselves so they are facing just one person. Choose a spot to stand as the facilitator so that the group can easily hear and see you.

1. Tell the group that they are about to have a series of 30-second conversations with several different partners, about some different questions related to the day.
2. Establish a method for regathering the group's attention; chimes and "If you can hear my voice, clap your hands once!" are two effective techniques.
3. Ask the first question, reminding students that each person in the pair will have 30 seconds to respond, so one minute total.
4. Get the group's attention and instruct one of the circles to remain stationary while the other circle rotates a given number of people in a certain direction. For example, "Outer circle, rotate two people to your right."

5. Repeat this process with the same or a different question. When complete, do another rotation to mix up the pairs again.

6. Continue for several rounds.

7. Sample questions include:

   • How well are we working as a team? What did you see today that supports your idea?

   • Do you feel like you are able to contribute to the group fully? Why or why not?

   • What would help your group to improve in teamwork?

   • What about working in a group can you apply outside of class?

   • What do you like about problem-solving challenges?

   • What is hard about problem-solving challenges?

Lesson 31

Problem Solving
Decision Making

ACTIVITIES ⚽

1. Team Tag (10 minutes)
2. Knot My Problem (30 minutes)
3. Debrief: Pass the Knot (5 minutes)

MATERIALS ✍

- Long rope tied in a loop
- One fleece ball per group of four students. Each ball should be a different color (red, green, blue, etc.)

---

1. TEAM TAG (10 MINUTES)

Objective: To tag everybody on the other teams while keeping at least one group member in the game.

Setup: Use an obstacle-free space such as half of a basketball court or a field with defined boundaries.

Framing: Say to students: "It is important to have leaders who see the big picture. When we are focused on the small tasks that we need to do, we need leaders to help us see the big picture."

1. Ask students to form small groups of four players.
2. Give each small group a different colored fleece ball (blue team, red team, green team, etc.).
3. Explain to the group that they can tag anyone but their own teammates.
4. In this version, if someone gets tagged, they stop wherever they are but can get back into the game if their color of fleece ball is tossed to them.
5. If a player with the team ball is tagged, he or she needs to toss it to another player on their team and then have it tossed back to return to the game.
6. Players are not allowed to interfere with other teams' fleece ball.
7. Play several rounds allowing a short planning time in between.

Facilitation Tips
None.

2. KNOT MY PROBLEM (30 MINUTES)

Objective: To work as a group and untangle a long rope starting coiled, then tangled, then ending as a large circle.

Setup: Clear a large, open space in your classroom. Tie the long rope into a closed loop (square knot works well). Loosely coil the rope so that the *large* loops are slightly separated from one another.

Framing: Say to students: "Have you ever felt like you were in a jam? A situation where you were faced with a particular problem or decision and were unclear about what to do? As a group you have a problem to solve."

1. Instruct the students to stand in a circle and place the coiled rope in the center of the circle.
2. Have students reach down and place one hand on the rope across from where they are standing.
3. Next, ask students to stand up and pull rope back slightly. The rope will now be in a giant "knot."
4. Tell students that the goal of the activity is to untangle the knot without taking their hands off the rope. They will be finished when the rope is in one big circle.

Safety Check

Emphasize self-care and being mindful of one another and of turning wrists and shoulders, as well as of people pulling the rope quickly, which could cause rope burn.

Facilitation Tips

If the class is unsuccessful after a long period of time, 10 to 15 minutes, allow them to break and then regrip one connection that the group mutually agrees upon, and then resume their attempt to untangle. A successful attempt will result in one large circle. Leave the ropes tied in a circle for the next activity, asking students to remain holding it.

3. DEBRIEF: PASS THE KNOT (5 MINUTES)

Objective: To reflect on behaviors that helped/hindered the group to solve today's problems.

Setup: If the rope was untied from the last activity, retie two ends of rope together to form a circle. Use any knot that will hold (square knot works well). Have the group stand or sit in a circle loosely holding the knotted rope.

Framing: Say to students: "As the knot in the rope is passed to you, please share one behavior that helped our group to solve the initiative and one behavior that hindered our ability to solve the initiative today. Once you have shared, pass the knot to the person to your left."

1. Have students share their response to the question above, then pass the knot when they are finished.
2. If a student wants to pass, you can come back to them at the end.

Safety Check
Do not allow students to tug on the rope or hold firmly, as they could get rope burn.

Problem Solving

Competition vs. Cooperation

ACTIVITIES ⚽

1. Thumb Wrestling (5 minutes)
2. Rob the Nest/Share the Wealth (30 minutes)
3. Debrief: Hoop Scoot (10 minutes)

MATERIALS ✍

- Five hula hoops
- Fleece balls or other tossables, about 20 total

---

1. THUMB WRESTLING (5 MINUTES)

Objective: To score as many points as possible in a one-minute round.

Setup: Ask participants to pair up with someone nearby.

Framing: Say to students: "This is an activity that is all about the scoring! Your goal is to score as many points as possible in the 60-second round. You are competing against the other pairs."

1. Explain to the group that they are going to thumb wrestle with their partner, and ask a volunteer to help you demonstrate what thumb wrestling looks like. Tell them very clearly that their goal is to score "as many points as possible" in the 60-second round.
2. Students should start when you say "Go" and stop when you say "Stop."
3. Time rounds for comparison to later attempts (whether it is 60 seconds, 30, or 90 doesn't really matter; short is most important).
4. A point is scored when the thumb of your opponent is pinned down even for a moment.
5. Students should remember to keep track of their score.
6. After the first round, ask students how many points they all have. Challenge them to get even more points on the second round.
7. Conduct a second (third or fourth) round of thumb wrestling until they start figuring out that this can be viewed as a cooperative activity instead of a competitive activity.
8. Go around and share points between rounds so students can hear if some pairs are beginning to work cooperatively.

Safety Check

Be careful of wrists and fingers; no extreme twisting or bending.

Facilitation Tips

If no one makes the cooperative connection, try prompting them by asking them to remember what the goal of the activity is. Ask if they are accomplishing that goal.

Take a moment to ask each pair what their score(s) were. Generally they'll all reply with something like "Two to nothing" or "Three to one." Tell them they'll have another round and that their goal is to at least double their score. This may help them make the transition from competition to collaboration.

Optional Questions:

- What was the goal of the activity?
- Why were your first scores so low?
- Why was there a disconnect between the goal and your first few tries?

2. ROB THE NEST/SHARE THE WEALTH (30 MINUTES)

Objective: To quickly collect or dispose of tossable items.

Setup: Set out five hula hoops, one at each corner of a square and one in the center of the square. The sides of the square should be about 25 feet. Place 20 fleece balls or other tossables inside of the center hoop. Divide the class into four equal groups and have each group stand next to one of the corner hoops.

Framing: Say to students: "Each small group represents a different neighborhood within town. Each neighborhood wants to gather the resources they need to have a safe and fun place in which to live."

1. Tell the students that the goal of the activity is to be the first team to get five items into their hoop (nest).
2. Team members must start each round with a foot inside of their hoop.
3. Each team's hoop must be accessible during the round, i.e., no moving or blocking the hoop.
4. Only one person may leave the team's nest at a time.
5. Only one item can be retrieved at a time. Items may be retrieved from either the center hoop or any other team's nest.
6. Once a team has gotten five items to their nest, they should raise their hands up and call out, "We win! We win!"
7. Give the teams a few minutes to plan before beginning the first round and time in between each round to revise their strategy.
8. After playing multiple rounds, change the rules to the Share the Wealth variation. The rules are: each group starts with five items in their nest; the goal is to be the first team to empty their nest; rules from Rob the Nest about carrying objects and number of people leaving the nest remain the same.

9. Consider stopping action at different points during this game to review ABCDE with the groups. Send a representative from each group to have a conference to talk to each other.

Safety Check

Make sure the play area is free from obstacles.
Remind students to treat everyone with respect—keep each other safe!

Facilitation Tips

Changing the number of objects can influence the outcome. Increasing the distance between hoops will change the amount of movement associated with this activity.

Optional Questions:

- What conflicts arose during this activity?
- Have the group resolve some of the conflicts; can they get to a win-win solution?

3. DEBRIEF: HOOP SCOOT (10 MINUTES)

1. Using the five hula hoops from the last activity, ask students to evenly distribute themselves in the hoops. If they need to have one foot in and one foot out, that is fine.
2. Let students know we will be playing a modified version of Have You Ever that we played earlier in the year. The difference is that, instead of one spot per person, we have five hula hoops.
3. As you say statements, students should find another hoop if the statement is true for their experience.
4. It is important to stress that this is a walking activity.
5. Remind students that there is no pushing other students out of the hoop. They must calmly find a new hoop.
6. Sample statements include:
   - I learned something new about cooperation today.
   - I knew right away how to score higher points in thumb wrestling.
   - I liked the Rob the Nest version of the game.
   - I liked the Share the Wealth version better.
   - I need more practice with cooperation activities to get better at it.
   - I think cooperation is harder than competition.

Lesson 33

Problem Solving
Efficiency and Effectiveness

ACTIVITIES ⚽

1. Evolution (5 minutes)
2. Toxic Waste (30 minutes)
3. Debrief: Pipe Cleaners (10 minutes)

MATERIALS ✍

- Toxic Waste kit
- Three to four pipe cleaners per student

---

1. EVOLUTION (5 MINUTES)

Objective: To have everyone evolve during the game through several levels to a Supreme Being.
Setup: Have students circle up.
Framing: Say to students: "Remember the game rock-paper-scissors?" (Review the game if necessary.) "In this game, we will use rock-paper-scissors to help each other evolve from being little eggs to being Supreme Beings!"

1. The characters in the game are:
    Egg—students crouch down and can waddle around.
    Chicken—students put their hands under their armpits, flap their "wings," and make chicken sounds.
    Dinosaur—students put their hands above their heads and make roaring sounds.
    Supreme Being—the group can make up their own motion and character (or see Facilitation Tips)
2. Everyone starts out as an Egg. Eggs will waddle up to other Eggs and engage in a round of rock-paper-scissors.
3. Whoever wins that round of play gets to evolve to the next character. For example, the winning Egg would become a Chicken.
4. Chickens then look for other Chickens with whom to play rock-paper-scissors, and so on.
5. Only like characters can play rock-paper-scissors with like characters. One exception is the Supreme Being.

6. Once students have reached the Supreme Being status, they may approach any character at any level and play a round of rock-paper-scissors. The Supreme Being keeps their status whatever the outcome, but if the lesser character wins, that character gets to evolve.

7. Supreme Beings will need to look out for those less evolved to help get the whole class to the Supreme Being status.

8. Once everyone has fully evolved, the activity is over.

Safety Check

Students with knee problems could be uncomfortable crouching like Eggs. Permit them to stand in an alternative position.

Facilitation Tips

The Supreme Being motion can be something light and fun. Choosing Diana Ross (of the Supremes) as the Supreme Being may get a giggle; the motion can be singing a verse of "Stop in the Name of Love." The game can end with the song being sung by the entire class.

This game is silly! Trust that once you start playing, they will get into it. Vary the level of silliness according to the readiness of your participants.

2. TOXIC WASTE (30 MINUTES)

Objective: To work as a group to transport a can of toxic waste out of the Radiation Zone and empty it into the neutralization bucket.

Setup: Use the rope to create a circle at least eight feet in diameter on the ground to represent the toxic waste Radiation Zone. Fill a bucket with the colored balls (toxic waste) and place it in the center of the Radiation Zone. Place the neutralization bucket at the other end of the classroom. Organize desks and tables as obstacles along the path. Give the students the remaining materials to make a "toxic waste transport system."

Framing: Say to students: "The challenge is for the entire group to transfer the toxic waste from the small blue bucket into the red bucket where it will be 'neutralized.' The waste will blow up and destroy the world in 25 minutes if it is not neutralized. Only the equipment provided may be used. You must all be connected to the transport system for it to work. The rope circle represents the Radiation Zone emanating from the toxic waste in the can. No one may step into the Radiation Zone. During transport, everyone must maintain a similar distance from the toxic waste. Getting too close to the toxic waste may lead to severe injury, such as loss of a limb or eyesight, for the remainder of the activity. Should you choose to accept this mission, your object is to save the world and do so without injury to any group members. You will have a mandatory five-minute planning and practice session before the 20-minute countdown begins."

1. If someone breaches the Radiation Zone, indicated by the circle, enforce an appropriate penalty. This might include loss of limbs (hand behind back) or loss of sight (eyes closed) that lasts for the rest of the activity.

2. This penalty may also be applied if students lose contact with the transport system or if they get too close to the toxic waste during transport.
3. The group must take five minutes of planning before they can proceed. Then start the clock and indicate it is time for action (20 minutes).

Safety Check

Students should be mindful when using the rubber band/bungee to avoid any snapping.

Facilitation Tips

The solution involves stretching the rubber band/bungee with the cords to sit around and grab the toxic waste bucket. Then, with students pulling on their cord and with good coordination and care, the toxic waste bucket can be lifted, moved, and tipped into the empty neutralizing bucket. If the group spills the waste entirely, make a big deal about catastrophic failure (everyone dies), invite them to discuss what went wrong and how they can do better, and then refill the container and let them have another go. *Do not* restart the time—the group continues with the amount of time remaining.

3. DEBRIEF: PIPE CLEANERS (10 MINUTES)

1. Pass out three to four pipe cleaners per person.
2. Ask students to sculpt a moment from the lesson where they thought the group was particularly effective.
3. Go around the circle and ask students to describe the moment to the class and show their sculpture. If they are not done with their sculpture, they can pass and you can come back to them at the end.

Lesson 34

Goal Setting
Long-Term Goals

ACTIVITIES ⚽

1. Transformer Tag (5 minutes)
2. Pathways (30 minutes)
3. Debrief: Small Group Questions (10 minutes)

MATERIALS ✍

- 30 spot markers (use those from Keypunch set)
- Markers
- Masking tape
- Graph paper (optional)

---

1. TRANSFORMER TAG (5 MINUTES)

Objective: To warm up and consider how changes happen quickly.

Setup: Clear a large space where students can run around.

Framing: In this game, players regularly change teams, let go of their connections to one side, and join their opponents.

1. Show the group the two body positions they will be using in this game: one hand on top of the head, or one hand on their hip. Ask each person to choose one of their positions, but tell them not to do it yet. Your free hand will serve as "bumper" and "tagger."
2. Explain that as soon as everyone is ready, you will begin the game with calling out, "Transform!" Each player will take his or her selected position. Those with their hands on their head will try to tag those with hands on their hip, and vice versa. If tagged, a player then "transforms" and begins trying to tag former teammates.
3. Play continues until everyone is on one team and there is no one left to tag.
4. Have rematches as time and interest allow, pointing out that group members may change their starting position for each match.

Safety Check

Remind the class about what constitutes an appropriate tag (gentle touch, and tag only shoulders or below).

Facilitation Tips

For small spaces, use boundaries to designate a safe play space and/or only allow heel-to-toe walking.

2. PATHWAYS (30 MINUTES)

Objective: To navigate a path, using your team and memory to get to the end.

Setup: Prepare spot markers by putting an X, using masking tape, on the numbered side of each spot marker that is not on the Pathway. Either leave the appropriate numbers (if using spot markers from your Keypunch set) on your spot markers or use masking tape to number them, as in the diagram below. You will need to create the "Pathway of the Life I Want" that your students will follow. To help create this Pathway, map it out on a piece of paper (graph paper works well) and devise a route that will use 30 spots and begin at the entrance side of the area and end at the exit side. Don't share this with your students! Lay your spots out, numbered or X side down, in a 5 x 6 grid. Solutions can involve forward, side, or backward movements. Diagonal moves or moves that skip rows are not allowed. The more moves you create in your solution, the more difficult the activity will be.

E N T R A N C E	1	2	X	16	17	18	E X I T
	X	3	4	15	14	X	
	X	6	5	X	13	X	
	X	7	X	11	12	X	
	X	8	9	10	X	X	

Framing: Say to students: "How do you know what the right path of life is? How do you make choices about long-term goals? Let's see if as a group we can help one another with finding the correct Pathway in this game."

1. Tell the group that the challenge for this activity is to find the correct Pathway. This is accomplished by discovering the predetermined sequence of steps to get one person from the entrance to the exit.

2. To do this they will select a spot, turn it over, and read the number to determine if it is the correct choice. If correct (as represented only by the next number in the sequence—if four was the last overturned, then the correct number would be five), step on the spot and repeat

the process with another adjacent spot. If they have made an incorrect choice, they must exit the Pathway.

3. Only correct spots will remain turned over showing the number. All incorrect choices result in the wrong-sequenced number being turned back over before exiting the Pathway. (Hint: if students can remember the numbers they have already looked at, it will prevent future mistakes and will aid in correct turns, like the childhood game of memory.)

4. One person at a time is allowed to enter the Pathway. If they make a correct choice, they may continue.

5. People on the Pathway may only move forward, backward, or sideways. Diagonal moves or moves that skip rows are not allowed.

6. After the framing, group members may position themselves anywhere around the Pathway to assist the person on the Pathway and to observe. No verbal or written communication with the person on the Pathway is allowed. Nonverbal communication is allowed.

7. The person on the Pathway should not be touched.

8. The group will rotate turns so the last person in goes to the back of the line.

9. The activity ends when the group is able to get one person all the way through the Pathway.

Facilitation Tips
Optional Question:
How did you feel about trying to find the path even though you were set back?

3. DEBRIEF: SMALL GROUP QUESTIONS (10 MINUTES)

Ask students to discuss the following in groups of three:
"Today was about adapting to new situations and making the best choices we can in the moment. How can you do that outside of this class in your own life? What skills did you use to stay on the path? How can you use these skills later in school?"

Lesson 35

Problem Solving

Final Group Challenge

ACTIVITIES ⚽

1. Great Egg Drop (30 minutes)
2. Debrief: Full Value Contract (15 minutes)

MATERIALS ✍

- Straws (20 per small group of four to six students)
- Masking tape (36 inches per group)
- Egg (one per group)
- Garbage bag, paper towels, and a trash can for cleanup
- Flip chart paper
- Markers
- Full Value Contract

---

1. GREAT EGG DROP (30 MINUTES)

Objective: Small group challenge.

Setup: Open the garbage bag and tape it to the floor on the far side of the open space. (Students will be dropping their protected eggs from six feet high onto this spread-out bag.) You can place a chair next to the garbage bag for students to stand on to drop their egg.

Framing: Say to students: "For our final challenge we will use our creativity, out-of-the-box thinking, communication skills, and a sense of friendly competition."

1. Separate the group into teams of four to six people.
2. Give each team an egg, 36 inches of tape, 20 straws, flip chart paper, and markers.
3. Explain to the students that the challenge of this activity is to construct a container for their eggs that will prevent them from breaking when dropped from a height of six feet.
4. Tell students that the egg must be inside the container somehow (the straws cannot be used as a nest on the floor that the egg drops into) and should be able to withstand a drop from six feet.
5. Also explain that the second part of the challenge is to create a name and a one- to two-minute commercial for their container that lets everyone know why theirs is the best, most protective,

and most efficient support system ever made. They can make posters for their commercials and/or act them out for the whole group—whichever they choose.

6. Tell the teams that they have 20 to 30 minutes to develop their support container/network and commercial. Each team will present their one- to two-minute commercial just before dropping their eggs.
7. After designated construction time, gather everyone in a large group. Have students sit on the floor of the room in a horseshoe shape so that there is sort of a stage near the egg drop (chair/garbage bag, etc.).
8. Have the first team present their commercial and drop their egg. Each team should have a representative drop the team's egg from a height of about six feet.

Facilitation Tips

Occasionally an egg will break. Use this as an opportunity to discuss trial and error.

Optional Questions:

What were you surprised by during this activity and why?

2. DEBRIEF: FULL VALUE CONTRACT (15 MINUTES)

1. Pull out the group's Full Value Contract.
2. Have students pair up and discuss which aspect of the Full Value Contract they think the group most improved on over the course of the year. Additionally, have each pair discuss where they each individually think they most improved.
3. Bring the group back together and ask each pair to report out.

Lesson 36

Closure

Review Semester and Celebrate Highlights

ACTIVITIES ⚽

1. Tool Kit (20 minutes)
2. Warm Fuzzies (15 minutes)
3. Letter to Self (10 minutes)

MATERIALS ✍

- Blank paper
- Envelopes (one per student)
- Assorted pens and markers

---

1. TOOL KIT (20 MINUTES)

Objective: To identify specific skills and knowledge that students acquired through the program and which they can transfer to their following school year.

Setup: Have students break into groups of three or four. Pass out blank paper and writing utensils.

Framing: Say to students: "We have done a lot together this year. After some reflection and discussion in a small group, you are going to make a tool kit for yourselves. This kit will contain tools that represent important concepts, lessons, and skills that you have learned and that will help you as you go on to your next year at school."

1. In your small groups, discuss key skills, concepts, and other learning gained during the SELA program.
2. Each group should develop a tool kit containing metaphorical tools (four to six different tools) that represent these key skills, concepts, etc. Give students some examples such as: "One tool could be a giant eraser, because we learned that being creative sometimes means changing how you approach something." Or "One tool would be a ladder because we progressed a little further each week in our teamwork."
3. Have each group pick their top one to two tools from all their ideas to present to the larger group. They should have one drawing for each tool.
4. Ask students to come back to one large circle and present in their small groups their one or two tools to put in the larger toolbox. (If you have a box, hula hoop, etc., that students can place their tools in, it will help continue the metaphor.)

2. WARM FUZZIES (15 MINUTES)

Objective: To give and receive positive feedback from other students.
Setup: Have students sit in a circle with a blank sheet of paper and a colored pen. Include yourself in the circle.
Framing: Explain to the students how much you've learned and appreciated in working with the group and that learning doesn't come only from the teacher or activities, but also from students in the class. This activity offers an opportunity to find out what students learned and appreciated from each other.

1. Have each student write their name at the top of the page. You can use your own sheet as a sample to show how large your name should be.
2. Let students know they will pass papers in a clockwise fashion so each student has someone new each pass.
3. Ask students to write down one thing they learned from or appreciated about the student whose page they have in front of them. Offer a few examples: "You were great at including everyone in the problem solving." "You helped us to refocus when we got distracted." "You made me laugh when we would get frustrated during a challenge to lighten the mood." "You are really organized."
4. Remind students to be appropriate and also to be brief in their comments so there is not a backup of sheets.
5. Give students a moment to record their thoughts and then prompt them to pass the papers clockwise. If there is a small pileup, *remind students to be brief*, but it will work itself out as they write and pass.
6. Continue the writing and rotation until everyone receives their own sheet.
7. Allow students a few minutes to read what others have said about them before proceeding to the next activity.

Facilitation Tips
Students sometimes get "stumped" with what to write. At the start of the activity, provide a few examples of appropriate statements to make.

3. LETTER TO SELF (10 MINUTES)

Objective: To record highlights and significant memories from the SELA program.
Setup: Hand out blank paper and an envelope to each student.
Framing: Explain that these will be mailed to them over the summer.

1. Have the students write their address on the envelope.
2. Tell students they are going to write a letter to themselves to remind their future self what was most important and valuable from the SELA program in terms of skills and competencies that they can use later.

3. Students are free to write as they wish, as the letters will not be read by you the teacher, yet the letters should reflect on students' experiences in the SELA lessons. Encourage students to be creative and expressive in their writing.

4. When students are done, they may seal the envelopes and hand them in.

Facilitation Tips

Be sure that students correctly complete their mailing address.

Appendix A
Have You Ever? Cards

Have You Ever . . . Been a big brother or sister?	Have You Ever . . . Been in the newspaper?	Have You Ever . . . Been on television?
Have You Ever . . . Grown your own vegetables?	Have You Ever . . . Been to a farm?	Have You Ever . . . Climbed a mountain?
Have You Ever . . . Received a trophy?	Have You Ever . . . Received an award?	Have You Ever . . . Helped a friend?

Have You Ever . . . Been camping?	**Have You Ever . . . Flown on a plane?**	**Have You Ever . . . Traveled out of the state?**
Have You Ever . . . Performed in a play?	**Have You Ever . . . Been to a concert?**	**Have You Ever . . . Traveled out of the country?**
Have You Ever . . . Been in a parade?	**Have You Ever . . . Sung in a chorus or a choir?**	**Have You Ever . . . Played a musical instrument?**

Have You Ever . . . Been on an athletic team?	**Have You Ever . . .** Volunteered?	**Have You Ever . . .** Been a role model to a younger child?
Have You Ever . . . Written a really good story?	**Have You Ever . . .** Snorted while laughing?	**Have You Ever . . .** Cooked an entire meal by yourself?
Have You Ever . . . Been paid for a job?	**Have You Ever . . .** Swum in the ocean?	**Have You Ever . . .** Gone to a beach?

Have You Ever . . .

Have You Ever . . .

Have You Ever . . .

Have You Ever . . .

Have You Ever . . .

Have You Ever . . .

Have You Ever . . .

Have You Ever . . .

Have You Ever . . .

Appendix B
Efficiency and Effectiveness Odometers

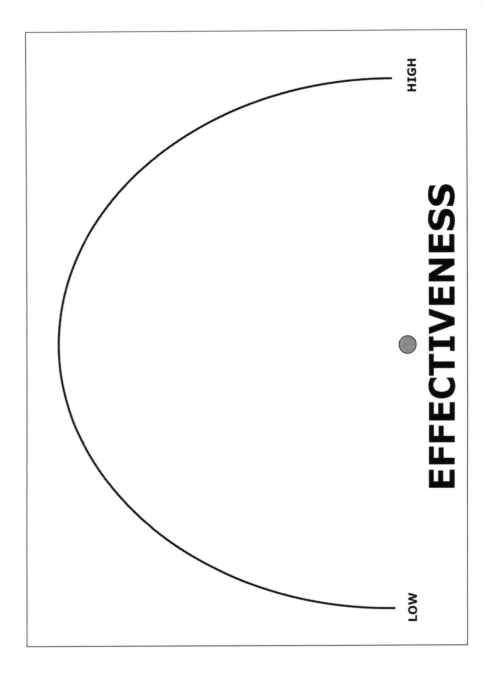

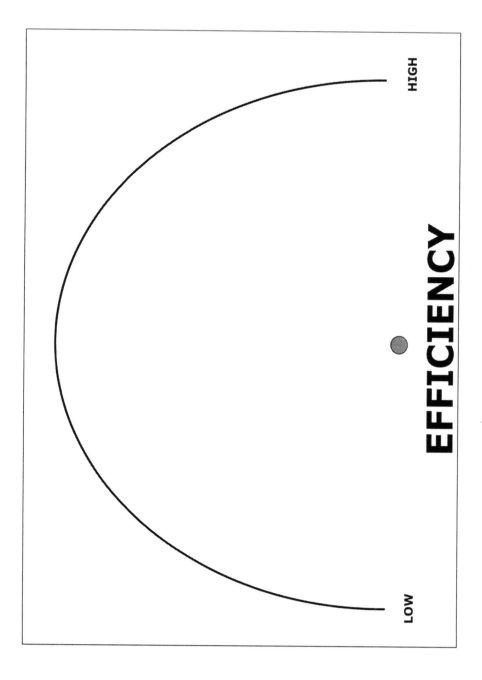

Appendix C
On Target Rules

ON TARGET RULES

Goal

Work as a team to earn as many points as possible in 90 seconds.

Rules

1. Buckets and lines cannot be moved.

2. Balls must be thrown into matching buckets from behind the line. (Earn one point per ball that is in the right bucket.)

3. Each ball must bounce at least one time before coming to rest in the bucket.

4. Each team decides the ratio it wants of ball Throwers and Retrievers.

5. The ball can only be tossed into the buckets by ball Throwers. Throwers must stand behind the line.

6. Loose balls can only be retrieved by the Retrievers. Retrievers can be anywhere.

7. Balls can be recycled after *all* the balls are in *all* the buckets.

Appendix D
Feelings Chart

Accepted	Afraid	Angry
Anxious	Ashamed	Bold
Bored	Brave	Calm
Cautious	Confident	Confused
Courageous	Crazy	Curious
Depressed	Determined	Disappointed
Disgusted	Eager	Ecstatic
Embarrassed	Energetic	Enraged
Excited	Exhausted	Flexible
Friendly	Frightened	Frustrated
Glad	Happy	Helpless
Hurt	Hysterical	Infuriated
Inspired	Jealous	Lonely
Loving	Mad	Mischievous
Miserable	Moody	Nervous
Optimistic	Overwhelmed	Panicky
Peaceful	Pessimistic	Proud
Pumped	Put Down	Relaxed
Restless	Sad	Scared
Shocked	Shy	Silly
Smart	Strong	Surprised
Suspicious	Tense	Upset
Vulnerable		

Appendix E
Warp Speed Rules

WARP SPEED RULES

. . . there are only three rules

1. Passing of the object must start and stop with the same person. (Whoever starts it must get it back to complete the cycle.)

2. The object must move sequentially from person to person. (Not everyone can touch it at the same time.)

3. Each player must have possession of the object as it moves through the cycle.

Appendix F
ABCDE Problem Solving

ABCDE PROBLEM SOLVING

When a group is making a decision that impacts everyone, remember to . . .

Ask

What is the problem/challenge the group is facing?

Brainstorm

What are the possible solutions?

Choose

Pick one idea.

Do it

Put your idea into action.

Evaluate

How did your idea work?
Do you need to choose a different idea?

Appendix G
SELA Skill Cards

Self-Awareness	**Healthy Relationships**	**Effective Communication**
Goal Setting	**Problem Solving**	**Community Building**
Decision Making	**Building Trust**	**Leadership**

Appendix H
Goal Mapping Worksheet

GOAL MAPPING

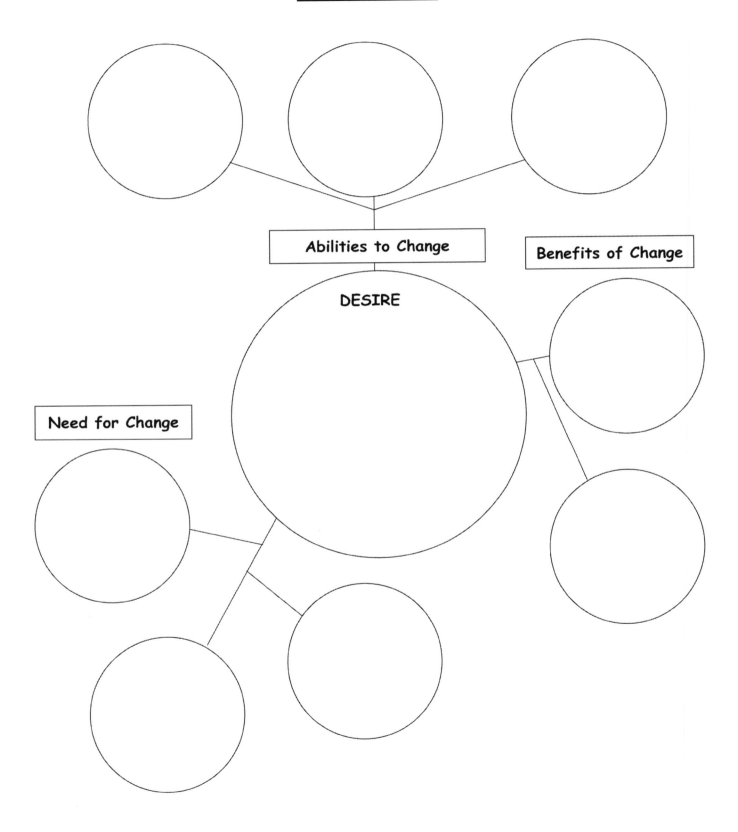

Appendix I
My Qualities Cards

**One of the qualities
I bring to this group is . . .
Looking out for others**

**One of the qualities
I bring to this group is . . .
Dedication**

**One of the qualities
I bring to this group is . . .
Good listener**

**One of the qualities
I bring to this group is . . .
Laughter/humor**

**One of the qualities
I bring to this group is . . .
Support group decisions**

**One of the qualities
I bring to this group is . . .
Help resolve conflict**

**One of the qualities I bring to
this group is . . .
Taking other people's
perspective**

**One of the qualities
I bring to this group is . . .
Analyzing problems
systematically**

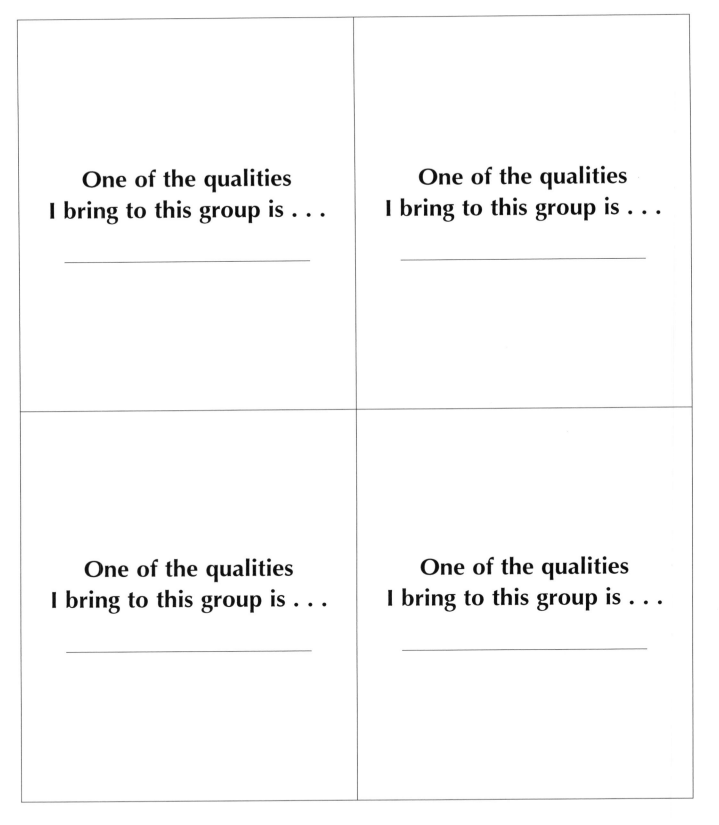

**One of the qualities
I bring to this group is . . .**

_____

**One of the qualities
I bring to this group is . . .**

_____

**One of the qualities
I bring to this group is . . .**

_____

**One of the qualities
I bring to this group is . . .**

_____

Appendix J
Keypunch Rules

KEYPUNCH RULES

- Spots and lines cannot be moved.

- Each number must be touched in numerical order, and all numbers must be touched.

- Only one person is allowed in the keypad area at one time.

- Each member of the team must touch at least one number.

- There is a five-second penalty for each rule violation.

- The time starts when the first person crosses the starting line.

- Time stops when the last person crosses back over the finish line (same as the start line.)

- You will have three attempts to score the fastest total team time possible.

Appendix K
Plus/Delta Worksheet

+ PLUS/DELTA Δ

Think back to what happened in Round 1 . . . in Round 2 . . . and in Round 3?

+ **Plus** Things you all did well	**Delta Δ** Things that need improvement
Give two **specific examples** of what the GROUP did well during the activity	What are two examples of what the GROUP can do to improve?

Appendix L
Back-to-Back Draw

BACK TO BACK DRAW

Round 1

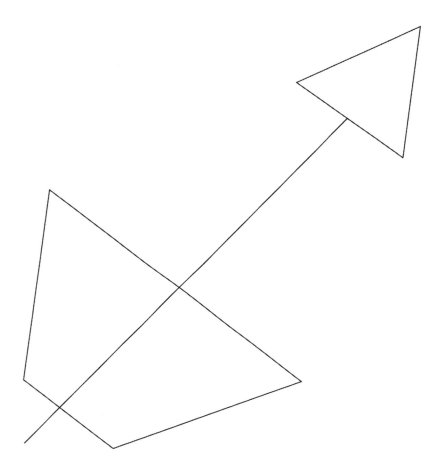

BACK TO BACK DRAW

Round 2

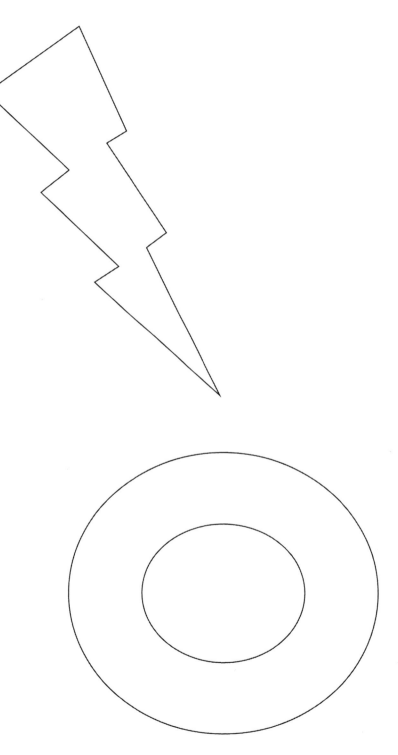

Appendix M
Original Source for Previously Published Activities

LESSON 1

Bumpity Bump Bump—No Props p. 60
Commonalities—Quicksilver p. 76
Categories—No Props p. 31

LESSON 2

Crosstown Connection—The Hundredth Monkey p. 64
What's in a Name—no source
Have You Ever—Adventure Curriculum for Physical Education: Middle School p. 19

LESSON 3

Knee Tag—The Hundredth Monkey p. 112
Comfort Zones—Adventure Curriculum for Physical Education: Middle School p. 48
Full Value Concepts—no source
Group Juggle—Quicksilver p. 201

LESSON 4

Full Value Speed Rabbit—no source
The Being—Youth Leadership in Action p. 60
Decision Thumbs—A Teachable Moment p. 80

LESSON 5

Look Up, Look Down—No Props p. 127
Robot—Adventure Curriculum for Physical Education: Elementary School p. 156
Paired Trust Walk—Quicksilver p. 229
Sherpa Walk—No Props p. 154
Debrief: Full Value Contract—no source

LESSON 6

Everybody Up—No Props p. 157
Trust Leans—No Props p. 140
Wind in the Willows—No Props p. 141
Pair Share—no source

LESSON 7

Hog Call—No Props p. 126
Trust Wave—No Props p. 134
Trust Run—Adventure Curriculum for Physical Education: High School p. 48
Woofs and Wags—no source

LESSON 8

Moonball—Quicksilver p. 176
On Target—Quicksilver p. 149
Odometer—A Teachable Moment p. 96

LESSON 9

Elevator Air—No Props p. 37
Communication Breakdown—no source
Nuggets—no source

LESSON 10

Creating a Feelings Chart—no source
Emotion Charades—no source
Balloon Trolleys—Quicksilver p. 147
Small Group Questions—no source

LESSON 11

Caught Ya Peekin'—No Props p. 188
Lego Statue—no source
Plus/Delta—A Teachable Moment p. 173

LESSON 12

Salt and Pepper—No Props p. 94
Turnstile—Silver Bullets p. 156
1, 2, 3 = 20—Adventure Curriculum for Physical Education: High School p. 237
Pass the Knot—no source

LESSON 13

Silent Lineup—Adventure Curriculum for Physical Education: Elementary School p. 199
Warp Speed—Cowstails and Cobras p. 83
Star Wars—Adventure Curriculum for Physical Education: High School p. 235
Continuum—Adventure Curriculum for Physical Education: Elementary School p. 199

LESSON 14

RPS World Championship—The Hundredth Monkey p. 173
Group Blackjack—no source
Change Up—Adventure Curriculum for Physical Education: Middle School p. 119
Deck of Cards—A Teachable Moment p. 172

LESSON 15

Who Am I?—no source
Virtual Slide Show—A Teachable Moment p. 237
Did Ya? Debrief—no source

LESSON 16

Gotcha FVC Review—no source
Stargate—Expanded Activity Guide p. 94
The Being Revisited—no source

LESSON 17

How Do You Do?—Adventure Curriculum for Physical Education: High School p. 30
I'm OK, You're OK Tag—Stepping Stones Activity Guide p. 50
Goal Mapping—no source
Gallery Walk of Goals—no source

LESSON 18

My Qualities—no source
Stepping Stones—Quicksilver p. 186
Small Group Questions—no source

LESSON 19

Velcro Circle—Adventure Curriculum for Physical Education: Middle School p. 49
Blind Shape—Cowstails and Cobras p. 81
Blind Polygon—Cowstails and Cobras p. 81
One Word Whip—no source

LESSON 20

Balloon Frantic—Silver Bullets p. 19
Protector—Stepping Stones Activity Guide p. 181
Pair Share—no source

LESSON 21

Everybody's Up—No Props p. 157
Levitation—No Props p. 142
Continuum—Adventure Curriculum for Physical Education: Elementary School p. 199

LESSON 22

Psychic Handshake—No Props p. 36
Orient the Square—Adventure Curriculum for Physical Education: Elementary School p. 203
Negotiation Square—Adventure Curriculum for Physical Education: Elementary School p. 246
Human Camera—No Props p. 123

LESSON 23

Goal Pair Share—no source
Mass Pass—Stepping Stones Activity Guide p. 177
Bucket Voting—A Teachable Moment p. 63

LESSON 24

Car and Driver—Adventure Curriculum for Physical Education: Elementary School p. 158
Don't Break the Ice—The Hundredth Monkey p. 72
Leadership Pi Chart—Stepping Stones p. 115

LESSON 25

Front/Back/Left/Right—The Hundredth Monkey p. 79
Instigator—No Props p. 185
Pitfall—Silver Bullets p. 24
Pitfall Objects—no source

LESSON 26

Your Add—No Props p. 173
Keypunch—Quicksilver p. 169
Plus/Delta—A Teachable Moment p. 172

LESSON 27

Circle the Circle—Silver Bullets p. 60
Portable Porthole—Adventure Curriculum for Physical Education: High School p. 54
Passenger, Crew, Captain—no source

LESSON 28

Triangle Tag—No Props p. 98
Alphabet Soup—Fastback—Stepping Stones Activity Guide p. 161
Tic-Tac-Toe—A Teachable Moment p. 91

LESSON 29

Back-to-Back Draw—no source
Bridge It—Silver Bullets p. 127
Headliners—no source

LESSON 30

Tarp Toss—no source
Turn over a New Leaf—no source
Concentric Circles—A Teachable Moment p. 76

LESSON 31

Team Tag—Stepping Stones Activity Guide p. 200
Knot My Problem—The Hundredth Monkey p. 118
Pass the Knot—no source

LESSON 32

Thumb Wrestling—Adventure Curriculum for Physical Education: Elementary School p. 163
Rob the Nest/Share the Wealth—Adventure Curriculum for Physical Education: Elementary School p. 248
Hoop Scoot—no source

LESSON 33

Evolution—No Props p. 175
Toxic Waste—Quicksilver p. 178
Pipe Cleaners—no source

LESSON 34

Transformer Tag—Quicksilver p. 91
Pathways—Adventure Curriculum for Physical Education: High School p. 63
Small Group Questions—no source

LESSON 35

Great Egg Drop—Youth Leadership in Action p. 94
FVC Debrief—no source

LESSON 36

Tool Kit—no source
Warm Fuzzies—no source
Letter to Self—A Teachable Moment p. 148

Appendix N
SELA Equipment Purchase Lists

COMMON SUPPLIES

- Blank paper
- Pens/pencils
- Assorted markers (including permanent markers for writing on balloons/masking tape)
- Masking tape
- Scotch tape
- Flip chart paper
- Index cards
- Assorted pipe cleaners (three to four per student)
- Scissors
- String
- Cardboard platform for "Bridge It" (Lesson 29)
- Straws
- Paper cups
- Egg (one for each four to six students)
- Garbage bags
- Quarter-inch bungee cord
- Playing cards (1 deck)
- Beach ball
- Two small tarps (6 x 8 or 8 x 10 feet)
- Balloons (two per student plus spares)
- Five hula hoops
- One "Matchbox" style toy car
- Three sets of 30 to 40 basic Lego building blocks (the sets must contain exactly the same pieces)
- Blindfolds/bandanas (one per student)
- Short ropes for start/end lines (clothesline, hardware-store-quality rope, or retired climbing rope)*
- Long rope (approximately 50 to 60 feet)*

*These ropes can be taken out of the specialty kits to be purchased from Project Adventure.

SPECIALTY SUPPLIES/KITS

Theses supplies can be more difficult to find.
The following websites sell these experiential materials/kits:
http://www.project-adventure.org/props
http://high5adventure.org/store/games-props/kits

- Fleece balls (one per student; assorted colors)
- Two rubber animals (e.g., chickens)

- Stepping Stones (one per student)
- Mass Pass Standard
- Keypunch set
- Alphabet Soup
- Toxic Waste (aka Object Retrieval)

Appendix O
SELA Logic Model

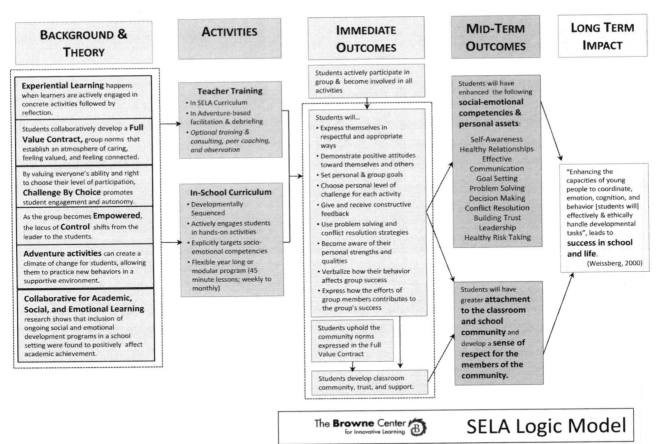

The **Browne** Center for Innovative Learning   **SELA Logic Model**

References

Aubry, P. (Ed.). (2009). *Stepping stones: A therapeutic adventure activity guide*. Beverly, MA: Project Adventure, Inc.

Cain, J., Cummings, M., & Stanchfield, J. (2005). *A teachable moment: A facilitator's guide to activities for processing, debriefing, reviewing and reflection*. Dubuque, IA: Kendall/Hunt.

Collard, M. (2005). *No props: Great games with no equipment*. Beverly, MA: Project Adventure, Inc.

Folan, N. (2012). *The hundredth monkey: Activities that inspire playful learning*. Beverly, MA: Project Adventure, Inc.

Panicucci, J. (2002). *Adventure curriculum for physical education: Middle school*. Beverly, MA: Project Adventure, Inc.

Panicucci, J. (2003). *Adventure curriculum for physical education: High school*. Beverly, MA: Project Adventure, Inc.

Panicucci, J., & Constable, N. S. (2003). *Adventure curriculum for physical education: Elementary school*. Beverly, MA: Project Adventure, Inc.

Rohnke, K. (1984). *Silver bullets: A guide to initiative problems, adventure games, and trust activities*. Beverly, MA: Project Adventure, Inc.

Rohnke, K. (1989). *Cowstails and cobras II: A guide to games, initiatives, ropes courses, & adventure curriculum*. Beverly, MA: Project Adventure, Inc.

Rohnke, K., & Butler, S. (1995). *Quicksilver: Adventure games, initiative problems, trust activities and a guide to effective leadership*. Dubuque, IA: Kendall/Hunt.

Youth leadership in action: A guide to cooperative games and group activities written by and for youth leaders. (1995). Dubuque, IA: Kendall/Hunt.

About the Author

Tara Flippo, M.A., is the youth and student programs director at the Browne Center for Innovative Learning (www.brownecenter.com) and the Clinical Faculty in Outdoor Education at the University of New Hampshire. She has been working with youth and educators alike for over two decades in school, camp, after-school, adventure, and educational settings. Tara holds a B.A. in outdoor experiential education from Hampshire College and an M.A. in social justice and outdoor experiential education from Vermont College. Prior to her role at the Browne Center, she was a manager and director for 8 years at Project Adventure (PA), Inc. In addition to her PA tenure, Tara has served as assistant director of an after-school program, course director for outward bound, diversity trainer, and contract facilitator at several northeast outdoor education organizations. She has worked extensively to bring experiential practices and innovative activities into youth development settings, positively impacting thousands of youth and educators.

Made in the USA
Middletown, DE
25 September 2017